Jump Start Your Career
in Technology & IT
in about 100 Pages

# Table of Contents

Let's Start !

# Introduction

Microsoft Visual Studio 2013 is the new version of the popular integrated development environment for building modern, high-quality applications for a number of platforms such as Windows, the web, Microsoft cloud, tablets running Windows 8, and Windows Phone devices.

The key word in Visual Studio 2013 is "productivity." Microsoft well knows that developers spend most of their time writing code, so the new version adds many tools to increase productivity and to help developers be faster and more efficient. The .NET Framework 4.5.1 does not introduce any new features to managed languages such as Visual Basic and Visual C#; on the other side, lots of enhancements have been made to the integrated development environment.

In this book you will learn what's new in Visual Studio 2013 for the code editor, for the debugger, for Windows 8.1, for the web and the cloud (including the new integrated support for Windows Azure subscriptions), and much more. There are so many improvements to support new and updated technologies that you will easily understand why a new release of Visual Studio was important after only one year.

Visual Studio 2013 ships with the following editions: Ultimate, Premium, Professional, and Test Professional, plus the free Express editions. Most features described in this book require Visual Studio 2013 Professional, but some of them require Visual Studio 2013 Ultimate, which is the most complete edition available. I will specify where the Ultimate edition is required. For a full comparison, you can look at this page in the Visual Studio portal from Microsoft. You can also download a fully-functional, 90-day trial of Visual Studio 2013 Ultimate (and other editions) from the Visual Studio Downloads page. The Express Editions are lightweight, free of charge editions of specific development environments for non-professional developers, hobbyists, and students that can be used even for commercial purposes.

Available products are Visual Studio 2013 Express for Windows Desktop (which you use to build WPF, Windows Forms, and Console apps), Visual Studio 2013 Express for Windows (which you use to build Windows Store apps for Windows 8.x), and Visual Studio 2013 Express for Web (which you use to build apps and sites for the web and the cloud). You can download the Express Editions from the same download page as above.

It is worth mentioning that Visual Studio 2013 allows building apps for Windows Phone 8, but not for Windows Phone 7.x. If you still need to build apps for Windows Phone 7.x, you will need to use Visual Studio 2012 and the Windows Phone 7.1 SDK. Visual Studio 2013 can be safely installed side-by-side with Visual Studio 2012. Also, Visual Studio 2013 allows opening most Visual Studio 2012 projects without modifying files for a perfect backward compatibility. A full list of conversion scenarios is provided in the MSDN documentation.

# Chapter 1 Synchronized Settings and Notifications

Most developers work on different computers, such as desktop workstations, laptops, and servers. In most situations, developers install Visual Studio onto each computer they work with. As you know, the IDE (integrated development environment) is customizable and allows adjusting a number of settings, such as adding buttons to toolbars, changing colors, using different fonts, and so on. Before Visual Studio 2013, you had to adjust settings manually on every installation of Visual Studio, which requires more time and the risk of forgetting to change some settings. Visual Studio 2013 introduces *synchronized settings*, so that every time you make customizations in the environment, these will be automatically applied to the other installations of Visual Studio on different computers. This chapter explains how this new feature works and how you can customize your work environment just once.

## Sign in to Visual Studio

The first time you start Visual Studio 2013, you will be asked to specify a default profile, such as web programming, Visual Basic programming, general development, and other profiles from previous versions of the IDE. This is a step you've already taken many times, so I will not spend much time here. After selecting the profile, Visual Studio 2013 will ask you to sign in with a Microsoft Account (formerly known as Windows Live ID). A Microsoft Account is an email address based on one of the Microsoft providers such as Hotmail, Live, or Outlook. Figure 1 demonstrates this.

*Figure 1: Visual Studio 2013 asks you to sign in with a Microsoft Account.*

Signing in with a Microsoft Account is not mandatory; you will certainly be able to use Visual Studio without an email address. However, signing in is advantageous for the following reasons:

- You can take advantage of Synchronized Settings, as described later in this chapter.
- Signing in with a Microsoft Account permanently unlocks any Visual Studio Express you have installed.
- You will be automatically logged in to the Team Foundation Service account associated with your email address if you subscribed to this service.
- You can use a trial version of Visual Studio for 90 days instead of 30.
- Signing in will unlock Visual Studio if your Microsoft Account is associated with an MSDN subscription.

Assuming you already have a Microsoft Account, click **Sign in**. At this point you will be asked to enter your email address and password, as represented in Figure 2.

*Figure 2: Enter your credentials to get started.*

Click **Sign in**. At this point Visual Studio will recognize your profile and will show some information while preparing the environment for the first use (see Figure 3).

 *Tip: If you are installing Visual Studio 2013 for the first time on a computer but you already installed it onto a different machine, this is also the moment in which settings are synchronized. Information on how settings are synchronized is coming shortly.*

*Figure 3: Enter your credentials to get started.*

Visual Studio will also ask you to select one of the available development settings. If you have a previous version installed, such as Visual Studio 2012, the new IDE provides an option to import customizations from the previous version. You can choose from among General, JavaScript, SQL Server, Visual Basic, Visual C#, Visual C++, Visual F#, Web Development, and Web Development (Code Only). Choose the one that is closest to your interest. If you do not know what the best choice for you is, simply choose the General settings. Also, you will be able to select one of the available graphic themes (Light, Dark, Blue). Once signed in, Visual Studio shows your profile name and picture at the upper right corner of the IDE, including shortcuts to access your profiled detailed information and to connect to Team Foundation Service.

 *Note: Team Foundation Service is a cloud-based version of Team Foundation Server, the popular Microsoft platform for team collaboration. With Team Foundation Service you can host team projects and take advantage of source control and other team development tools wherever you are. Another important reason for signing into Visual Studio with a Microsoft Account is that the IDE automatically connects your account to the associated Team Foundation Service account. To create your Team Foundation Service account, visit http://tfs.visualstudio.com.*

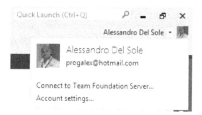

*Figure 4: The IDE recognizes the user and provides useful shortcuts.*

Once you have signed in, your settings are ready to be synchronized and shared across multiple computers.

# Synchronized settings

By default, Visual Studio 2013 can synchronize the following settings:

- Development settings. These are related to the development profile selected the first time you ran Visual Studio and can be changed by selecting Tools, Import and Export Settings, Reset All Settings.
- Theme settings, available in Options, Environment page, General tab
- Startup settings available in Options, StartUp
- All settings for the text editor available in Options, Text Editor
- All settings for fonts and colors available in Options, Environment, Fonts and Colors
- All default and custom keyboard shortcuts, available in Options, Environment, Keyboard
- Customized command aliases

 *Tip: Command aliases are a way to enter commands inside the Command window and allow opening dialogs or launch other tasks in Visual Studio, instead of using menus and menu items. The full list of built-in aliases is available at: http://msdn.microsoft.com/en-us/library/c3a0kd3x.aspx*

When you make changes or customizations, Visual Studio stores the aforementioned settings on the cloud, that is, on Microsoft servers, and associates those settings to the Microsoft Account you used to sign in. When you sign into Visual Studio with the same account on a different computer, the IDE downloads settings associated to your account and applies them to the active environment. Developers have been requesting this feature for a long time and finally Visual Studio 2013 solves the problem. This is just another example of how the cloud can make your life easier as a developer. Remember that synchronization works even if you have different editions of Visual Studio 2013, such as Ultimate, Premium, and Professional. Synchronization also applies to Express Editions, but it does not work if you have Express and non-Express editions on the same machine.

## Selective synchronization

You can disable settings synchronization or choose what you want to synchronize among the settings listed in the previous paragraph. To accomplish this, go to the **Tools** menu, then select the **Options** submenu, then the **Synchronized Settings** command. Figure 5 shows how the Options dialog appears at this point.

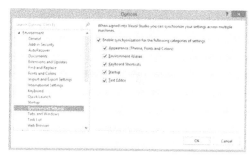

Figure 5: Enabling Synchronization and Settings Selection

The **Enable synchronization for the following categories of settings** check box is selected by default. If you unselect it, synchronization will stop until you explicitly re-enable it. You can also select one or more specific settings you want to synchronize, excluding settings you do not use. Click **OK** to apply your changes.

## Synchronization conflicts

For various reasons, synchronization across multiple machines can occasionally fail. If this happens, Visual Studio shows a message in the Notification Hub (see the next topic of this chapter). The MSDN documentation describes three possible solutions with some manual work. As a personal suggestion, turn synchronization off on the computer where it was not successful, and then sign out. Next, sign in again and turn synchronization on again.

# Notifications Hub

Visual Studio 2013 introduces a new concept of notifications. The goal is keeping the developer informed about product updates, extension updates, documentation updates, license issues, problems with the Microsoft Account, unresolved conflicts, and other errors. The IDE presents notifications to you via the Notifications Hub. The Notification Hub consists of a new tool window called Notifications and of a small flag icon (the Notifications button) placed near the Quick Launch bar, indicating the number of available notifications. To open the Notifications window:

1. Click the **View** menu.
2. Select the **Notifications** entry.

You can also click the **Notifications** button on the Quick Launch bar for faster opening. Figure 6 shows the Notification Hub.

*Figure 6: Enabling Synchronization and Settings Selection*

If you click the button, the Notifications tool window opens and shows a full list of notifications. You can expand the notification description and, in case the notification is about an update, you will be able to click a hyperlink that will redirect you to the download page. You can also ignore all notifications by clicking **Dismiss All**.

## Chapter summary

Among the new features in the IDE, Visual Studio 2013 makes it easy to share settings across multiple computers with Synchronized Settings; with this feature, most settings are saved to the cloud and applied to all of your other installations of Visual Studio. The Notifications Hub provides an easy way to download updates and to present information about other issues related to Visual Studio. Both features require you to sign into Visual Studio with your Microsoft Account, which also allows connecting to other Microsoft services without additional effort.

# Chapter 2 The Start Page Revisited

The Start Page has been an important place in Visual Studio since the early days. In the first versions of Visual Studio .NET, it was a static page containing shortcuts for creating new or opening existing projects, and a place to get the latest announcements from Microsoft. In Visual Studio 2010, the Start Page was completely redesigned; it was built upon Windows Presentation Foundation (WPF), providing not only a better integration with the IDE but also offering an opportunity to build completely customized entry points. In Visual Studio 2013 the Start Page has evolved even more, becoming the place where you start your work as well as learn about new and updated technologies.

## A new Start experience

An important concept behind the development experience in Visual Studio 2013 is that programmers should have everything they need inside the active page. The Start Page in Visual Studio 2013 has been reorganized based on this concept and includes not only shortcuts for working with projects, but also updated links to learning resources and announcements, all in one place. The Start Page has a dynamic layout, meaning that items inside the page are automatically rearranged when you resize the Visual Studio's window. Figure 7 shows how the Start Page appears when you run Visual Studio 2013.

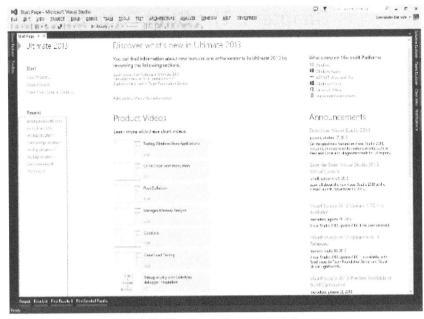

*Figure 7: The Start Page in Visual Studio 2013*

The Start Page is made of several areas, each described in the next sections of this chapter. Of course, you can still create and use custom start pages based on WPF (as you could do in Visual Studio 2010 and 2012) or you can disable the Start Page and choose a different entry point by using Tools, Options, Startup.

 *Note: This chapter does not cover how to build custom start pages. If you wish to create your own start page, read Start Pages in the MSDN documentation.*

What you find here is a description of what the Start Page contains and how it can make your life easier.

# Work with projects

 *Tip: In this and the next subsections, use Figure 7 as a reference to locate items in the Start Page.*

The first thing you probably do when you launch Visual Studio is open a project. On the left side of the Start Page you will find two areas related to working with projects, Start and Recent. Start contains shortcuts for creating new projects or opening existing ones, including from source controls platforms such as Team Foundation Server, Team Foundation Services, and GIT. Recent shows a list of recent projects; if you right-click the name of a project in the recent list, you will be able to open the project, open the containing folder, or remove the project from the list.

## Staying up to date: Announcements

The Announcements area shows news about product updates, new releases, events/conferences, and technical content from the various teams in Redmond working on Visual Studio. This is not new in the Start Page, but the behavior is different. First, you can no longer customize the source of the announcements; in the previous versions of Visual Studio you could specify a different RSS feed to show contents, but now the news channel cannot be changed. However, the news channel is now filtered with information that you actually need to stay up to date with new releases and with events focused on Visual Studio 2013.

## Learning

The Start Page now has more content for getting started with Microsoft technologies and with specific product features, as described in this section.

### What's new on Microsoft platforms

The **What's new on Microsoft platforms** area has shortcuts that make it easier to access the MSDN documentation for each of the most recent development platforms, operating systems, and collaboration platforms, such as Windows 8, Windows Azure, the web and ASP.NET, Windows Phone, Office, and SharePoint.

### Product Videos

The **Product Videos** area allows watching short instructional videos about specific features in the Visual Studio IDE. This is very useful for a better understanding of most of the new features, because the videos show them in action with practical examples. You might see the following text:

```
We have a lot of great content to show you, but we need your permission to get it and
keep it updated.
```

If you see this message, you need to click **Tools**, then click **Options**, and select **Startup** under the **Environment** node in the **Options** dialog; finally, check the **Download content every** check box. The default time interval is 60 minutes but you can increase or decrease the value. The reason for this is that Visual Studio uses your Internet connection to retrieve the list of available contents, so it needs your permission first.

### Discover what's new

At the top of the Start Page you can find an area that offers shortcuts to learn what new features are available in Visual Studio 2013, the .NET Framework 4.5.1, and Team Foundation Services. Such shortcuts will direct you to the appropriate page of the MSDN documentation.

## Chapter summary

With its revisited and dynamic layout, the Start Page in Visual Studio 2013 is more than a simple place where you create new projects or pick up existing ones; the Start Page is now the place where you can easily find all the learning resources and product releases you need to start building applications for the most recent Microsoft platforms.

# Chapter 3 Code Editor Improvements

The code editor in Visual Studio 2013 is one of the areas of the IDE where Microsoft made many investments. The goal is to make developers stay focused on the code they are writing, helping them perform common tasks more quickly and save time. This chapter describes new features in the code editor that will help you be more productive when writing code.

## Peek Definition

**Peek Definition** is a new feature that you can use to see and edit the definition of a class or class member inside a popup shown within the active code editor window. This helps you avoid the need to leave the active window in order to open the code file that contains the code block you need to edit. To understand how it works, create a new Console application then add a **Person** class like the following.

*Visual C#*

```csharp
public class Person
{
    public string FirstName { get; set; }
    public string LastName { get; set; }
    public DateTime DateOfBirth { get; set; }

    public override string ToString()
    {
        return string.Format("{0} {1}, born {2}",
            this.FirstName, this.LastName,
            this.DateOfBirth.ToShortDateString());
    }
}
```

*Visual Basic*

```vbnet
Public Class Person
    Public Property FirstName As String
    Public Property LastName As String
    Public Property DateOfBirth As Date

    Public Overrides Function ToString() As String
        Return String.Format("{0} {1}, born {2}",
            Me.FirstName, Me.LastName,
            Me.DateOfBirth.ToShortDateString())
    End Function
```

```
End Class
```

The **Main** method of the sample application simply creates a new instance of the **Person** class and assigns some values as in the following code.

*Visual C#*

```csharp
class Program
{
    static void Main(string[] args)
    {
        Person person = new Person();

        person.FirstName = "Alessandro";
        person.LastName = "Del Sole";
        person.DateOfBirth = new DateTime(1977, 5, 10);

        Console.WriteLine(person.ToString());
        Console.ReadLine();
    }
}
```

*Visual Basic*

```vb
Module Module1
    Sub Main()
        Dim person As New Person

        person.FirstName = "Alessandro"
        person.LastName = "Del Sole"
        person.DateOfBirth = New DateTime(1977, 5, 10)

        Console.WriteLine(person.ToString())
        Console.ReadLine()
    End Sub
End Module
```

Now suppose you want to make some edits to the **Person** class, such as renaming members or adding new ones. Right-click the type name (**Person** in our example) and select **Peek Definition**. As you can see from Figure 8, a pop-up appears showing the code of the **Person** class and the name of the code file where it is defined.

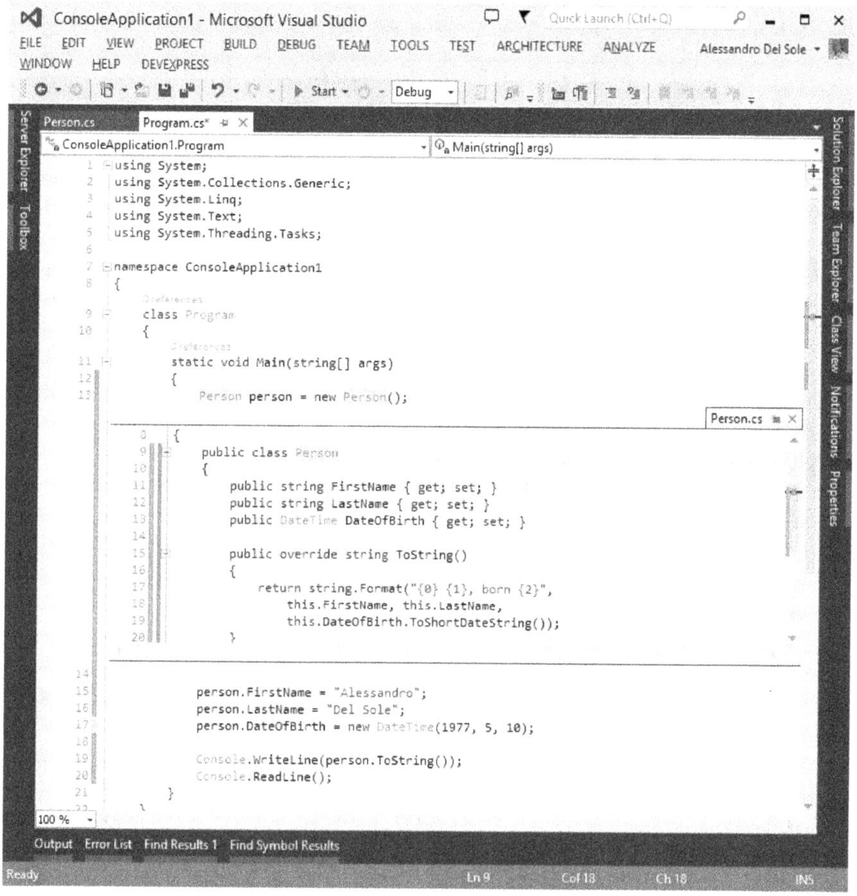

Figure 8: Editing Code with Peek Definition

Peek Definition offers a fully functional editor, so you can change your class (or member) definition according to your needs without leaving the active window. If you make any changes, these are immediately visible in the code that uses the class. When done, you can simply click the usual Close button to hide the Peek Definition content. This tool is a very useful addition, because it not only allows you to stay in the active editor window while making changes to a type, but it also makes it easier to find type definitions among millions of lines of code and thousands of code files.

## CodeLens

***Note: This feature is available only in the Ultimate edition.***

In many situations, you might need to know how many times an object has been used in your code and where. The previous (and current) versions of Visual Studio provide a tool called **Find All References**, which shows a list of references to an object inside a tool window called Find Symbols Results that you can invoke by right-clicking an object's name in the code editor and then selecting **Find All References**. Visual Studio 2013 makes a step forward, offering an additional integrated view of code references called **CodeLens**. Take a look at Figure 9, which shows the `Person` class definition inside the code editor.

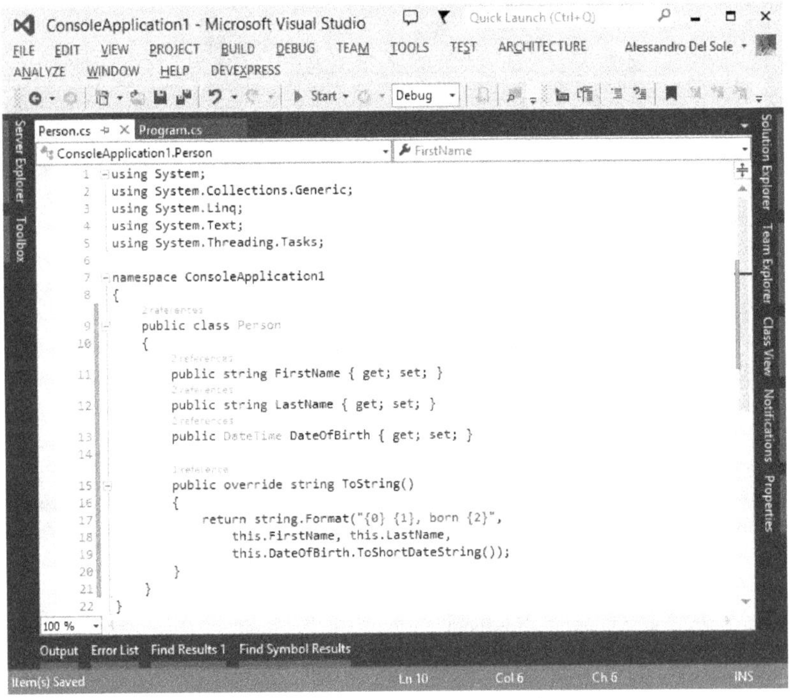

*Figure 9: Visual Studio 2013 shows the number of references for each type and member.*

As you can see, above each type and member name Visual Studio shows the number of references. If you click that number, a tooltip will show where the object is used; if you pass the mouse pointer over the line of code that contains the reference, another tooltip will show the full code block containing the reference (see Figure 10).

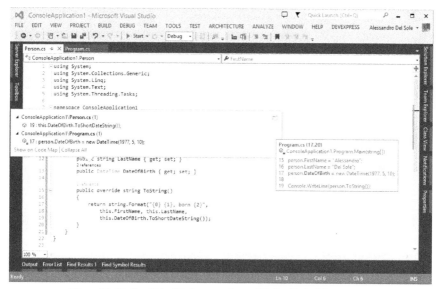

*Figure 10: Finding Object References from within the Code Editor*

CodeLens also shows the containing code file for each reference and the line number where the object is used, and allows fast navigation to the reference by double-clicking the line of code in the tooltip. Actually CodeLens does also an amazing job when your solution is under the source control of Team Foundation Server; in fact, it can show information about unit tests, passed tests, failed tests, and edits made by other team members.

# Enhanced Scroll Bar

In most of real world projects, code files are made of hundreds of lines of code, so finding specific code blocks inside a file can become difficult. In order to make it easier to browse very long code files, Visual Studio 2013 provides an improved scroll bar in the code editor window, known as enhanced scroll bar. Basically the scroll bar can show a map of the code (map mode) so that when you move the mouse pointer up and down, a magnifier shows a preview of the code block. This is very useful with long code files, if you want to see some code definition without jumping from one position to another in the code file.

To enable the map mode, right-click the scroll bar, then select **Scroll Bar Options**. In the **Options** dialog, locate the **Behavior** group and then select the **Use map mode for vertical scroll bar** option, as shown in Figure 11.

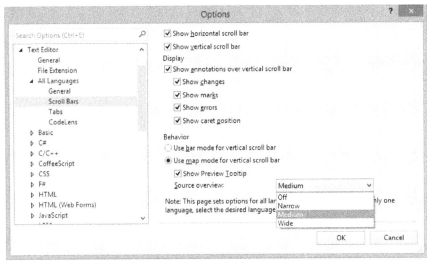

*Figure 11: Enabling the Map Mode for the Scroll Bar*

 **Note: Enabling the code preview is optional, but I encourage you to leave it selected. After all, it's the real benefit of this tool.**

You can also choose the size of the map by changing the value of the **Source overview** box. The default value is Medium, which is a good choice for most situations. Click **OK** to enable the map mode. When you go back to the code editor, you can see the scroll bar's new look. Figure 12 shows an example.

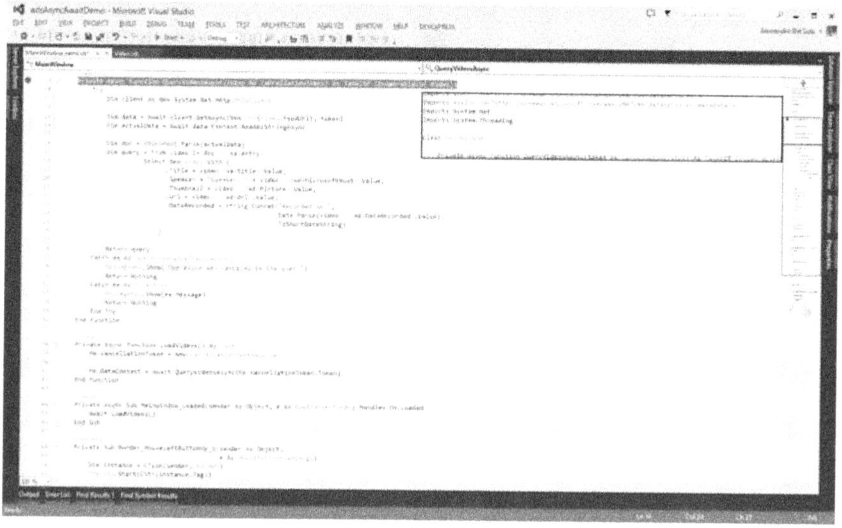

Figure 12: Browsing Code with the Scroll Bar in Map Mode

When you move the mouse pointer over the scroll bar, a tooltip shows a preview of the code for the current position on the map. A blue line indicates the cursor position, yellow dots indicate edited lines of code, and red dots represent breakpoints. You can simply revert to the classic scroll bar by going back to the scroll bar options and selecting the **Use bar mode for vertical scroll bar** option.

> *Tip: The enhanced scroll bar works with all languages supported by Visual Studio 2013. This means that when you enable the map mode, the scroll bar will show the map for every code file in any language until you disable it again.*

# Navigate To

Another key feature of Visual Studio 2013 in the code editor is called **Navigate To**. With this feature, you can easily find the definition of a type or member by placing the cursor on the type or member and then pressing **CTRL + ,** . Figure 13 demonstrates how Visual Studio 2013 shows types and members that contain the name selected in the code editor.

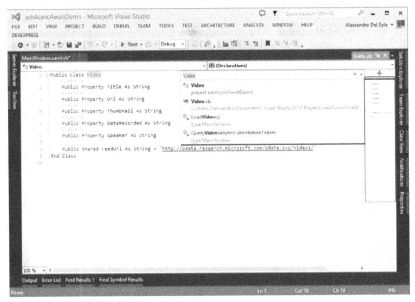

*Figure 13: Using Navigate To*

As you can see from Figure 13, a list of objects matching the type or member name is shown. You can press the up and down arrows on your keyboard to see every definition in the code editor without actually activating a window. As you can easily understand, Navigate To becomes particularly useful if you have multiple definitions of the same type in your solution and you want to go to its definition quickly.

## Chapter summary

The code editor in Visual Studio 2013 has been dramatically enhanced with new features that increase the developer's productivity by making it easier to complete common tasks. Peek Definition, integrated references, the enhanced scroll bar, and Navigate To give their contribution to make the new IDE a great place for writing code.

# Chapter 4 XAML IntelliSense Improvements

XAML (*eXtensible Application Markup Language*) is a markup language used to design the user interface in technologies such as Windows Presentation Foundation (WPF), Silverlight, Windows Phone, and Windows Store Apps for Windows 8. If you have experience with at least one of these technologies, which I assume you have, you know that Visual Studio, especially in the latest versions, offers a pretty good designer. In addition, Microsoft offers another tool called Expression Blend, which is dedicated to professional designers and allows working on the user interface with professional tools without interfering with the managed code behind. As a developer, most of the time you will work with Visual Studio. Although the designer has reached a very good level of productivity, a lot of times you will need to write XAML code manually; this is a very common practice, for example when you need to resize elements in the UI with exact proportions or when you need to assign styles or set data-bindings to controls. When you edit the XAML manually, you use the XAML code editor, which implements the IntelliSense technology, allowing you to write code faster. However, IntelliSense for XAML has always lacked some important points, such as recognizing available data sources and resources when using data-binding or assigning styles. Finally, Visual Studio 2013 addresses this issue and introduces a lot of new goodies into the XAML code editor.All of these new features are available to all technologies based on XAML.

 *Note: In the first preview of Visual Studio 2013, the new features in the XAML code editor were only available to Windows Store Apps. This limitation has been removed in the Visual Studio 2013 Release Candidate.*

## XAML IntelliSense for data-binding and resources

In Visual Studio 2013 you can now take advantage of IntelliSense when assigning a data source to a binding expression or when you assign a resource such as a style.

 *Note: This feature only works with data sources and resources that you declare in XAML. If you create an instance of a collection in managed code (at runtime), this cannot be recognized by the IntelliSense. It also works with design-time information that you declare through the d: XML namespace.*

Let's use an example to see how this feature works.

The goal of the example is declaring a collection of objects and binding the collection to the user interface using the new IntelliSense features. Data will be shown inside a **ListBox** control. Create a new WPF Application project called *Chapter 4*, for the sake of consistency. Add a new folder to the project and call it Model. Add a new class to the folder, called **Person**. The code for the new class looks like the following.

*Visual C#*

```csharp
namespace Chapter4.Model
{
    public class Person
    {
        public string FirstName { get; set; }
        public string LastName { get; set; }
        public int Age { get; set; }
    }
}
```

*Visual Basic*

```vb
Namespace Model
    Public Class Person
        Public Property FirstName As String
        Public Property LastName As String
        Public Property Age As Integer
    End Class
End Namespace
```

 *Note: While Visual C# automatically adds a namespace definition for each subfolder you create in the project, Visual Basic doesn't; it just recognizes objects under the root namespace. For the sake of consistency in both languages, we are adding a namespace declaration in Visual Basic so that we can use the same XAML with both.*

This is a very simple class with only three properties, but we are focusing on the new tools now rather than on writing complex code. The next step is adding to the Model folder a new collection of **Person** objects, called **People**. The code is the following.

*Visual C#*

```csharp
using System.Collections.Generic;
using System.Collections.ObjectModel;

namespace Chapter4.Model
{
    //add a using System.Collections.ObjectModel; directive
    public class People: ObservableCollection<Person>
    {
        public People()
        {
            Person one = new Person {LastName="Del Sole",
                                     FirstName="Alessandro", Age=36};
            Person two = new Person { LastName = "White",
                                      FirstName = "Robert", Age = 39};
```

```
            Person three = new Person { LastName = "Red",
                                        FirstName = "Stephen", Age = 42 };

            this.Add(one);
            this.Add(two);
            this.Add(three);
        }
    }
}
```

*Visual Basic*

```
Imports System.Collections.ObjectModel
Namespace Model
    Public Class People

        Inherits ObservableCollection(Of Person)
        Public Sub New()
            Dim one As New Person() With {.LastName = "Del Sole",
                                          .FirstName = "Alessandro",
                                          .Age = 36}
            Dim two As New Person() With {.LastName = "White",
                                          .FirstName = "Robert", .Age = 39}
            Dim three As New Person() With {.LastName = "Red",
                                            .FirstName = "Stephen",
                                            .Age = 42}

            Me.Add(one)
            Me.Add(two)
            Me.Add(three)
        End Sub
    End Class
End Namespace
```

The **People** class inherits from **ObservableCollection<Person>**. The constructor of the **People** collection creates three instances of the **Person** class, and populates them with sample data. The reason why we are creating a collection this way is that IntelliSense for XAML does not support collections created at runtime. Instead, with this approach we can declare the collection in the application's resources; every time a class is declared in the XAML resources, the constructor of the class is invoked, so in our case an instance of the collection is automatically created and populated when added to the XAML resources. Such an instance can then be data-bound to controls in the user interface. To do so, double-click the **MainWindow.xaml** file in Solution Explorer. When the designer and the XAML editor appear, first add the following namespace declaration within the **Window** tag.

```
<Window x:Class="Chapter4.MainWindow"
        xmlns="http://schemas.microsoft.com/winfx/2006/xaml/presentation"
        xmlns:x="http://schemas.microsoft.com/winfx/2006/xaml"
        xmlns:local="clr-namespace:Chapter4.Model"
        xmlns:controls="clr-namespace:Chapter4"
        Title="MainWindow" Height="350" Width="525">
```

This is necessary in order to reference the **People** and **Person** classes. The next step is declaring the data source as a resource, as shown in the following code.

```
<Window.Resources>
    <local:People x:Key="PeopleData"/>
</Window.Resources>
```

This is the point in which an instance of the **People** collection is declared, so we are ready to bind data to a **ListBox** control. As you know, in order to present information coming from a collection, the so-called item controls (like the **ListBox**) need to implement a **DataTemplate**. Let's add a **ListBox** and its **DataTemplate** without pointing to any data source, by writing the following code within the **Window** tag.

```
<Grid>
    <ListBox Name="PeopleBox" >
        <ListBox.ItemTemplate>
            <DataTemplate>
                <Border BorderBrush="Black"
                        BorderThickness="2">
                    <StackPanel Orientation="Vertical">
                        <TextBlock />
                        <TextBlock />
                        <TextBlock />
                    </StackPanel>
                </Border>
            </DataTemplate>
        </ListBox.ItemTemplate>
    </ListBox>
</Grid>
```

The data template simply presents the value of each property of the **Person** class with a **TextBlock** control, arranged inside a **StackPanel** container. The **Border** adorner is used for a better highlighting inside the designer, but it is optional. For a full demonstration of the new IntelliSense features, we can also add a new style for **TextBlock** controls. In Solution Explorer, double-click the **App.xaml** file. Within the **Application.Resources** tag, add the following style, which allows presenting text in red and with different size and weight for the current font.

```
<Application.Resources>
    <Style x:Key="MyTextBlockStyle" TargetType="TextBlock">
        <Setter Property="Foreground" Value="Red"/>
        <Setter Property="FontSize" Value="16"/>
        <Setter Property="FontWeight" Value="SemiBold"/>
    </Style>
</Application.Resources>
```

Now you are ready to test the new amazing IntelliSense for XAML.

## IntelliSense for data-binding

Switch back to the MainWindow.xaml file locate the **ListBox** control. As you know, item controls are populated by assigning their **ItemsSource** property with an instance of a collection, either at design-time (with XAML code) or at runtime (in managed code). We previously declared a data source as a resource, so a Source binding expression is needed to assign it as the **ItemsSource** property for the **ListBox**. To understand the benefit of XAML IntelliSense at this point, type the following code (not just copy/paste).

```
<ListBox Name="PeopleBox"
         ItemsSource="{Binding Source={StaticResource PeopleData}}">
```

After you type **StaticResource**, you will see how the IntelliSense will show a list of available objects that can be used for data-binding, as demonstrated in Figure 14.

*Figure 14: IntelliSense for Data-Binding in Action*

Select the **PeopleData** object to finalize data-binding. As in every other scenario where you write code, IntelliSense will help you complete the expression while you type. You can also select the data source with the arrows on your keyboard and then press **Tab**.

 *Tip: If you have multiple data-bound controls in the Window, you might want to bind the parent container's DataContext property instead (in this case the Grid) and then assign the ItemsSource property with the {Binding} expression.*

Similarly, you can bind **TextBlock** controls to properties of the collection with the help of IntelliSense, as demonstrated in Figure 15.

Figure 15: IntelliSense shows properties that can be data-bound.

This is a tremendous benefit for several reasons. First, you can write code faster. Secondly, you do not need to remember the name or the casing of properties, thus minimizing the risk of typos. The complete code of the **ListBox**'s data template is the following.

```
<DataTemplate>
    <Border BorderBrush="Black"
            BorderThickness="2">
        <StackPanel Orientation="Vertical">
            <TextBlock Text="{Binding LastName}"/>
            <TextBlock Text="{Binding FirstName}"/>
            <TextBlock Text="{Binding Age}"/>
        </StackPanel>
    </Border>
</DataTemplate>
```

## IntelliSense for resources

The next step is using IntelliSense to assign resources. We previously defined a style that must be now assigned to each **TextBlock** control in the Window. The code for the first **TextBlock** looks like the following. You might want to type the style assignment manually in order to see the XAML IntelliSense feature in action.

```
<TextBlock Text="{Binding LastName}"
           Style="{StaticResource MyTextBlockStyle}"/>
```

As it happened for data-binding, when you are assigning the **StaticResource** expression the IntelliSense will show available resources, as shown in Figure 16.

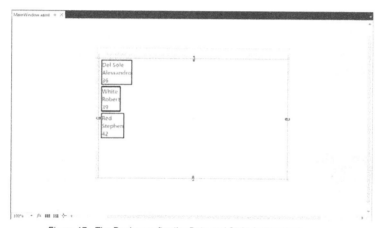

```
100%   ▾  ƒx ▦ ▦▦ ⟷ ◁
□ Design   ↑↓   ▤ XAML  ▣
     7          <local:People x:Key="PeopleData"/>
     8        </Window.Resources>
     9      <Grid>
    10          <ListBox Name="PeopleBox" ItemsSource="{Binding Source={StaticResource PeopleData}}">
    11            <ListBox.ItemTemplate>
    12              <DataTemplate>
    13                <Border BorderBrush="Black"
    14                        BorderThickness="2">
    15                  <StackPanel Orientation="Vertical">
    16                    <TextBlock Text="{Binding LastName}"
    17                               Style="{StaticResource }"/>
    18                  </StackPanel>
    19                </Border>                          ▤ MyTextBlockStyle
    20              </DataTemplate>                       ⚟ ResourceKey
    21            </ListBox.ItemTemplate>
100 %   ▾  ◁
```

Figure 16: IntelliSense shows available resources for the specified control.

It is worth mentioning that, in the case of styles, IntelliSense will only show styles valid for the control that you are working on, either defined in the application or defined in the .NET Framework or SDK extensions. This is an additional benefit, since you not only will avoid errors and will write code faster, but you will be also be picking up only resources that are specific for the selected element of the user interface. For the sake of completeness, Figure 17 shows how the designer looks at this point.

Figure 17: The Designer after the Data and Style Assignments

You can run the application by pressing **F5** to see how it displays data.

# Go To Definition

**Go To Definition** is a feature that you already know from the managed code editor. With this feature, you can right-click an object's name, select **Go To Definition** from the context menu, and see how the object is defined in the Object Browser window, if it is a built-in object from the .NET Framework, or in the appropriate code file if it is an object you wrote. This feature is now available to the XAML editor too, as demonstrated in Figure 18.

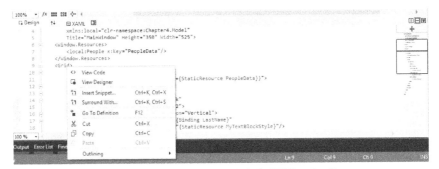

*Figure 18: Go To Definition is now available in the XAML code editor.*

 **Tip: The keyboard shortcut for Go To Definition is also F12 in the XAML code editor.**

Go To Definition is available for the following objects:

- Resources
- System types
- Local types (custom controls)
- Binding expressions

Let's walk through every object to see the different behavior of Go To Definition.

## Resources

In an XAML-based application, resources can be of two types: resources defined in an assembly (from .NET, from the SDK, or from a 3rd party library) and resources defined in the current application. In the first case, Go To Definition will open the Object Browser window pointing to the specified resource definition. For example, in the sample application created previously, place the cursor on the `MyTextBlockStyle` assignment in any of the `TextBlock` controls, then right-click and select **Go To Definition** (see Figure 19).

Figure 19: Go To Definition Over the Style Defined in the Sample Application

At this point, the code editor will open the definition of the resource at the exact position in the appropriate code file; in our case, the style definition inside the App.xaml file. As you can see (Figure 20), the cursor is placed at the beginning of the definition and the `Style` tag is selected.

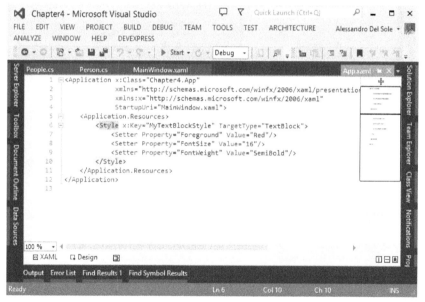

Figure 20: Go To Definition opens the resource definition at the exact position.

## System Types

Go To Definition works with types defined in the .NET Framework and SDK extensions. Since the source code of these types is not available, Visual Studio shows the definition inside the Object Browser window. For example, if you select Go To Definition on the `Grid` control in the MainWindow.xaml file of the sample application, the Object Browser will be opened, showing the control's definition (see Figure 21).

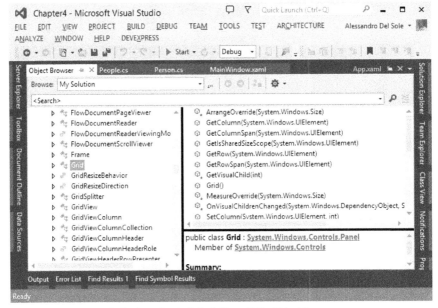

*Figure 21: Seeing a Control's Definition with the Object Browser*

## Local Types

Go To Definition has a particular behavior with local types; these are user controls and custom controls created by developers.

 *Note: This is not a book about WPF and other XAML-based technologies, so I will not cover the difference between user controls and custom controls in detail. As a hint, user controls are the result of the composition of existing controls; custom controls extend existing built-in controls with additional functionalities in code, and provide templating, theming, and styling entry points. For further information, read the Control Authoring Overview in the MSDN Library.*

To understand how it works, let's make some edits to the sample application. In **Solution Explorer**, right-click the project name, select **Add New Item**. Then, in the **Add New Item** dialog, select the **User Control (WPF)** template and name the new control **CustomBoxControl.xaml** (see Figure 22).

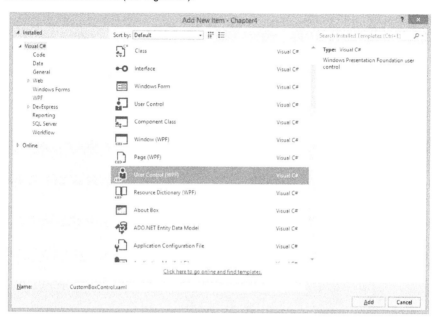

*Figure 22: Adding a New User Control*

Cut and paste the `ListBox` definition from MainWindow.xaml to the new control, and repeat this step for the `local` XML namespace declaration. Finally, add a local resource that points to the **People** collection as you did in MainWindow.xaml. The full code of the user control looks like the following.

```
<UserControl x:Class="Chapter4.CustomBoxControl"

xmlns="http://schemas.microsoft.com/winfx/2006/xaml/presentation"
            xmlns:x="http://schemas.microsoft.com/winfx/2006/xaml"
            xmlns:mc="http://schemas.openxmlformats.org/markup-
compatibility/2006"
            xmlns:d="http://schemas.microsoft.com/expression/blend/2008"
            mc:Ignorable="d" xmlns:local="clr-namespace:Chapter4.Model"
            d:DesignHeight="300" d:DesignWidth="300">
    <UserControl.Resources>
        <local:People x:Key="PeopleData"/>
    </UserControl.Resources>
```

```xml
<Grid>
    <ListBox Name="PeopleBox"
             ItemsSource="{Binding
             Source={StaticResource PeopleData}}">
        <ListBox.ItemTemplate>
            <DataTemplate>
                <Border BorderBrush="Black"
                        BorderThickness="2">
                    <StackPanel Orientation="Vertical">
                        <TextBlock Text="{Binding LastName}"
                                   Style="{StaticResource
                                   MyTextBlockStyle}"/>
                        <TextBlock Text="{Binding FirstName}"
                                   Style="{StaticResource
                                   MyTextBlockStyle}"/>
                        <TextBlock Text="{Binding Age}"
                                   Style="{StaticResource
                                   MyTextBlockStyle}"/>
                    </StackPanel>
                </Border>
            </DataTemplate>
        </ListBox.ItemTemplate>
    </ListBox>
</Grid>
</UserControl>
```

In MainWindow.xaml, add the following XML namespace to include the user control.

```xml
xmlns:controls="clr-namespace:Chapter4"
```

Then, add the user control as follows.

```xml
<Grid>
    <controls:CustomBoxControl/>
</Grid>
```

If you did everything correctly, the designer now should still look like in Figure 17. Now, right-click **CustomBoxControl** inside the **Grid** and select **Go To Definition**. As you can see (Figure 23), Visual Studio 2013 opens the Find Symbol Results window and shows two results, one for XAML and one for managed code.

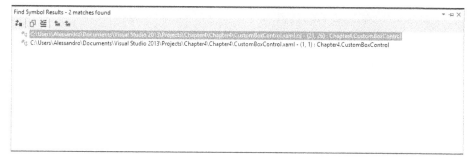

*Figure 23: Adding a New User Control*

The reason is that user controls (and custom controls as well) are made of two components, the XAML file defining the user interface and a code-behind file. You can then double-click the file you need and see the appropriate definition. The Find Symbol Result is a good choice, because you can also see the line number where the definition begins.

## Binding expressions

Go To Definition also works with binding expressions. For instance, you can right-click the name of the data source or of the bound property inside a **Binding** expression and select Go To Definition. With data sources (collections) defined as static resources, Go To Definition moves you to the definition of the resource; with data sources defined in managed code, Go To Definition attempts to make a full symbol search in the code, showing search results in the Find Symbol Results window. In the case of data-bound properties, Go To Definition moves you to the code of the class that exposes such a property.

# Automatic closing tag

When you add an item in XAML, the code editor automatically adds the closing tag. For instance, when you add a **<Button>** tag, Visual Studio adds the matching **</Button>** tag. This is not new, since it is the normal behavior in the earlier versions. The new feature is that if you add the slash before the > symbol in the first tag, the closing tag is automatically removed. In other words, in this code:

```
<Button Width="100" Height="50" Click="Button_Click" Name="Button1" Content="Click
me!"></Button>
```

If you type the slash before the > symbol, it automatically turns into the following code.

```
<Button Width="100" Height="50" Click="Button_Click" Name="Button1" Content="Click
me!"/>
```

This is another way the editor can help you write code faster.

## IntelliSense matching

Continuing its purpose to make your coding experience better, Visual Studio 2013 adds another feature to the XAML code editor, known as IntelliSense matching. Basically, when you start typing the name of a control or resource, the IntelliSense will help you find the appropriate control as you type, even if you enter the wrong characters. For example, Figure 24 shows how IntelliSense understands you need a **StackPanel** even if you are typing it incorrectly.

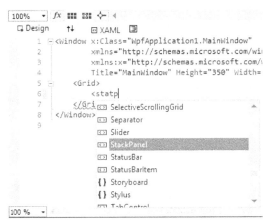

*Figure 24: IntelliSense Matching makes it easy to select controls as you type.*

IntelliSense does an excellent job, depending on how many identifiers can match what you are typing. For instance, in a Windows Store App, if you type **Abbb** it will suggest the **AppBar** control, which is probably your choice.

## Better support for comments

A common issue in previous versions of Visual Studio is that when you add a comment to a code block containing another comment, it causes the code editor to show an error message. Figure 25 shows how Visual Studio 2012 handles this kind of situation.

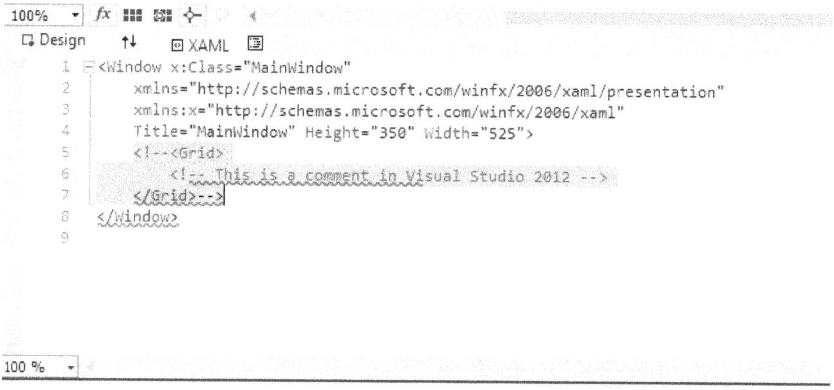

```
100%  ▼ fx ▦ ▦ ✛ ⯈ ◀
  ⊡ Design  ↑↓  ⊡ XAML  ▣
  1  ⊟ <Window x:Class="MainWindow"
  2        xmlns="http://schemas.microsoft.com/winfx/2006/xaml/presentation"
  3        xmlns:x="http://schemas.microsoft.com/winfx/2006/xaml"
  4        Title="MainWindow" Height="350" Width="525">
  5        <!--<Grid>
  6           <!-- This is a comment in Visual Studio 2012 -->
  7        </Grid>-->
  8   </Window>
  9
100 %  ▼ ◀
```

*Figure 25: Visual Studio 2012 does not recognize nested comments correctly.*

The problem was that the code editor did not recognize comment closing tags correctly. Visual Studio 2013 addresses this issue, so when you add a comment to a code block containing another comment, the entire code block gets commented, as demonstrated in Figure 26.

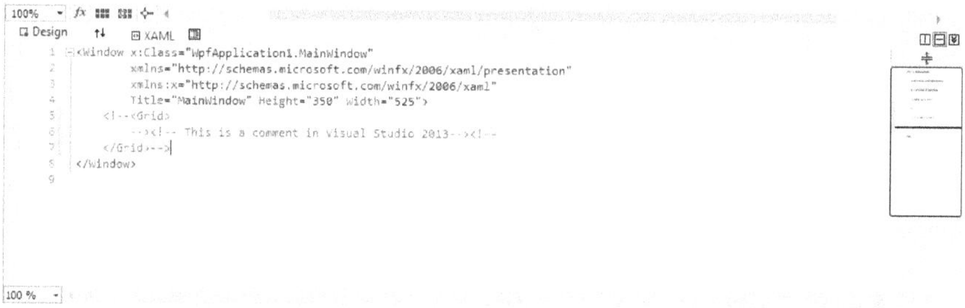

*Figure 26: Visual Studio 2013 correctly recognizes nested comments.*

# Reusable XAML code snippets

Reusable code snippets for IntelliSense have been a very popular feature since Visual Studio 2005, but have always been limited to managed languages, XML, and HTML/JavaScript in version 2012. With code snippets you can take advantage of a huge code library offered by Visual Studio or create your own code snippets, so that it is easier to reuse your code with the support of IntelliSense. The need of code snippets for XAML has always been very strong, so many developers used different techniques to store their reusable code. I wrote myself an extension for Visual Studio 2010 to support XAML code snippets. Visual Studio 2013 makes another step forward, introducing built-in support for code snippets in the XAML code editor.

To use code snippets, simply right-click in the code editor and select **Insert Snippet** or **Surround With**, as shown in Figure 27.

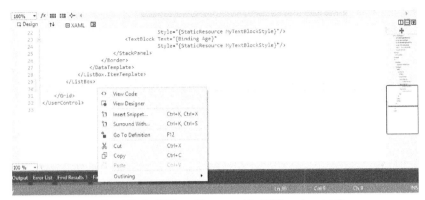

*Figure 27: Visual Studio 2013 provides support for XAML code snippets.*

At this point, a list of available code snippets appears. You can select the code snippet you need from the list and the related code will be placed there (see Figure 28).

*Figure 28: Selecting a Code Snippet from the List*

 **Note: This chapter is based on Visual Studio 2013 RTM released to the MSDN subscribers in October, 2013. In this release only one XAML snippet is supplied. At the time of this writing, we cannot predict if additional snippets will be provided, or if you will only be able to import your own, custom code snippets. This chapter does not explain how to build custom code snippet files, which is out of its scope. However, you can read this _interesting article_ from Tim Heuer, which explains XAML code snippets from creation to deployment.**

You can manage code snippet files with the Code Snippets Manager tool (available from the Tools menu), as you already did for other languages. This is the place where you can import, remove, and view detailed information about code snippet files. By adding XAML code snippets, Visual Studio 2013 bridges the gap with code editors for other languages.

# Chapter summary

Without a doubt, adjusting the user interface and supplying data-bindings manually in XAML code is a very common task in any XAML-based technology, including WPF, Silverlight, Windows Phone, and Windows Store Apps, despite the existence of specialized tools for designing. Visual Studio 2013 finally provides important improvements to the XAML code editor, such as IntelliSense for recognizing data sources and styles; Go To Definition for system types, local types, custom, and user controls; commenting nested code blocks; better handling of closing tags, and IntelliSense matching to help you select controls quickly; and reusable code snippets, finally added to XAML completing the availability of this tool to all of the supported languages.

# Chapter 5 Visual Studio 2013 for the web and Windows Azure

Programming for the web is the core business for many companies and developers. Creating websites means making an application available to potential customers worldwide through the Internet or providing internal portals or departmental applications through a local Intranet. Because of the importance of the web in a programmer's life, cloud computing platforms are becoming more and more important every day. With Windows Azure, Microsoft has released one of the most powerful and complete cloud infrastructures ever. With a platform like Windows Azure you no longer need an in-house data-center, removing the need of purchasing physical servers and paying for their maintenance; with Windows Azure, you only pay for services you actually use. This chapter does not explain what ASP.NET and Windows Azure are, nor does it explain how to create applications for both platforms; that's the goal of other resources. Instead, here we focus on how the new tooling available in Visual Studio 2013 makes programming for the web and the cloud an even more amazing experience with a deeper integration with the IDE.

 *Note: The .NET Framework 4.5.1 introduces some new features to ASP.NET. If you want to learn about what's new, you can visit the <u>appropriate page</u> in the MSDN Library. Here you learn about new features in the IDE for ASP.NET, not about the runtime.*

## What's new in the IDE for ASP.NET

Visual Studio 2013 introduces new tools and updates the existing environment for web development with ASP.NET. This chapter focuses on the most important features that you must know, as they will change the way you create web applications.

### One ASP.NET: A new, unified experience

In the past, Microsoft released several technologies for creating web applications, like Web Forms, ASP.NET Dynamic Data, and MVC. Similarly, a number of frameworks and libraries were released, such as jQuery, jQuery Mobile, Web API, and Windows Identity Foundation. You could choose among several kinds of project templates in order to build web applications and add references to your desired frameworks later. Visual Studio 2013 dramatically simplifies this process by introducing the so-called **One ASP.NET**, which provides a unified development experience and makes it easy to use any of the available platforms, as well as making libraries interchangeable. But what does One ASP.NET mean in practice? To understand what it is, open Visual Studio 2013 and select **File**, **New Project**. Select the **Web** templates folder. As you can see from Figure 29, now there is only one project template.

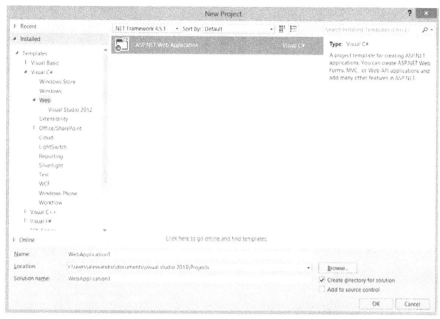

*Figure 29: One ASP.NET also means simplifying a project's creation.*

Unlike in the past, where you had to choose among a number of several project templates, now you have only one template. Don't be scared of this; in the next steps you will learn the reasons behind this feature and how to take advantage of it. For backward compatibility, you can still create web applications using templates inherited from Visual Studio 2012. You can simply expand the **Web** template folder and select the **Visual Studio 2012** subfolder (which is visible in Figure 29). You will see the classic list of available project templates based on Web Forms, MVC, and Ajax. Let's focus on One ASP.NET and double-click the single project template. At this point Visual Studio 2013 will show a new dialog, represented in Figure 30.

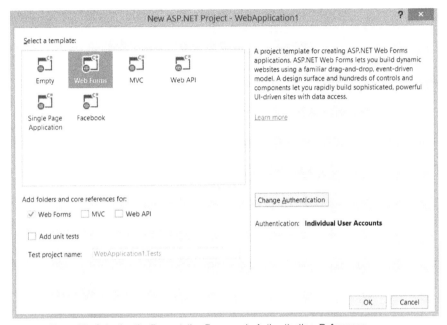

*Figure 30: Selecting the Presentation Framework, Authentication, References*

It's becoming clearer why the new approach is called One ASP.NET. In one place, you can:

- Select the presentation framework, such as Web Forms or MVC.
- Select a ready-to-use application stub, such as the Single Page Application or the Facebook application templates.
- Choose the authentication model: anonymous, Individual (ASP.NET), Windows (for Windows domains), Organizational (based on Active Directory, Office 365, and Windows Azure Active Directory).
- Add unit tests.
- Add folders and references to libraries that are specific to other frameworks; for instance, in a Web Forms application you can use MVC libraries and vice versa.

This new way of creating web applications gives you an opportunity to work with multiple kinds of libraries, taking full advantage of all the libraries from ASP.NET 4.5.1. Also, One ASP.NET simplifies the process by adding references for you. Experimenting with Web Forms, MVC, and other project templates is left to you as an exercise. Let's now take a closer look at new features from the IDE.

## Scaffolding for Web Forms

Scaffolding is all about data. Basically with scaffolding the IDE can generate view models and views based on a modeled data source (such as the ADO.NET Entity Framework); with scaffolding, Visual Studio generates for you pages that can read, insert, delete, or update data without you writing a single line of code. Technically speaking, Visual Studio generates a **controller**, which is a class containing the necessary code to perform C.R.U.D. (Create, Read, Update, Delete) operations against data, and pages to work with data (**Views**), one for each of the C.R.U.D. operations. Scaffolding is not a new concept in the ASP.NET development; it was first introduced with ASP.NET MVC. The good news is that Visual Studio 2013 brings scaffolding to Web Forms as well. This is possible because of the One ASP.NET experience; in fact, Visual Studio injects the appropriate MVC dependencies into a Web Form project and then does most of the work for you. If you already used this technique in MVC projects, you will be familiar with most of the concepts.

 *Note: With Visual Studio 2008 and .NET Framework 3.5 Service Pack 1, Microsoft introduced ASP.NET Dynamic Data, an innovative way of creating modern, data-centric applications for the web. Dynamic Data is still available in later versions. The concept of scaffolding was the base of ASP.NET Dynamic Data, but what we mean today by scaffolding is pretty different, and is based on new frameworks, libraries, and implements different code-behind. For this reason, be sure you have clear that in this chapter we refer to scaffolding by indicating the MVC (and now Web Forms) implementations.*

To understand how scaffolding works, we will now create a sample ASP.NET application based on Web Forms, then we will add a reference to a database. Then we will use the new tooling in Visual Studio 2013 to generate data-bound pages without writing a single line of code. Before you continue, ensure you have downloaded and installed the following prerequisites:

- Microsoft SQL Server 2012 Express Edition, as the database engine required for data access. I recommend you download either the "With Tools" or the "With Advanced Services" editions that will also install SQL Server Management Studio Express for database management.
- The Adventure Works sample database from Microsoft. It can be downloaded for free from this page of the CodePlex website.

We assume that you already know how to install a database like Adventure Works to SQL Server, so let's go ahead.

### Create a sample project

First you will create a sample project. This is also the first time for you to see the One ASP.NET tooling in action. To create the project, follow these steps:

1. Select **File, New Project.**
2. Select the **Web** templates folder (see Figure 1).
3. Select the one **ASP.NET Web Application** and call the new project **ScaffoldingDemo.**
4. Click **OK.**
5. In the **New ASP.NET Project** dialog (take Figure 30 as a reference), select **Web Forms** as the presentation framework, then select the **MVC** checkbox.

6. For the sake of simplicity, change the authentication mode to anonymous. This is just for testing purposes; in a real world scenario you must select the appropriate authentication type according to your needs. To change the authentication, click **Change Authentication**, then in the **Change Authentication** dialog, select **No Authentication** (see Figure 31).
7. Click **OK** to create the project.

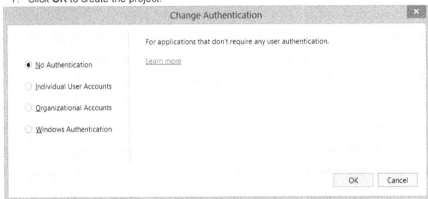

*Figure 31: Changing the Authentication Type*

 *Tip: For your curiosity or for real needs, while you are in the Change Authentication dialog, try to click on each option to see how you can implement different authentication types and how each type satisfies specific platform requirements.*

## Adding Data Connection and Entity Data Model

When the project is ready, in **Solution Explorer** right-click the project name, select **Add New Item**, and select the **Data** template folder. This is the point in which a data connection will be added, as demonstrated in Figure 32. Select the **ADO.NET Entity Data Model** item template; call the new model **AdventureWorks.edmx** and click **Add**.

*Figure 32: Adding a New Entity Data Model*

As you know, the Entity Data Model is based on the ADO.NET Entity Framework. In the **Entity Data Model** wizard, select the **Generate From Database** option first, then click **Next**. Click the **New Connection** button, then add a new connection that points to the **AdventureWorks** database. Figure 33 shows how the Connection Properties window will look like at this point; of course, you can have a different server name on your machine.

*Figure 33: Adding a New Entity Data Model*

At this point the Entity Data Model Wizard will show summary information for the newly created connection (see Figure 6). You can definitely leave unchanged the identifier for the connection settings or provide a different one (at the bottom of Figure 34).

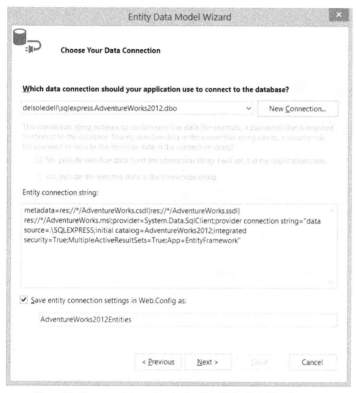

*Figure 34: Summary Information for the New Entity Data Model*

When you click **Next**, Visual Studio will ask you to specify the version of the Entity Framework you want to use, between 5.0 and 6.0 (default option). Leave unchanged the selection on version 6.0 and click **Next**. At this point you will need to specify the tables or views you want to add to the model. Just select the **Person** table, as we want to demonstrate concepts easily without having a complex data structure. Figure 35 shows how to make such a selection.

*Figure 35: Selecting Database Objects*

Click **Finish**. After a few seconds the Entity Data Model designer shows the .NET representation of the selected table (see Figure 36).

 *Tip: If you see a message that says "Running this template can potentially harm your computer," ignore it. Visual Studio always analyzes code snippets that execute actions against local resources, such as a database, including auto-generated snippets, but of course executing such actions is safe at this point.*

Before doing anything else, rebuild the project (**CTRL** + **Shift** + **B**) so that all references are updated.

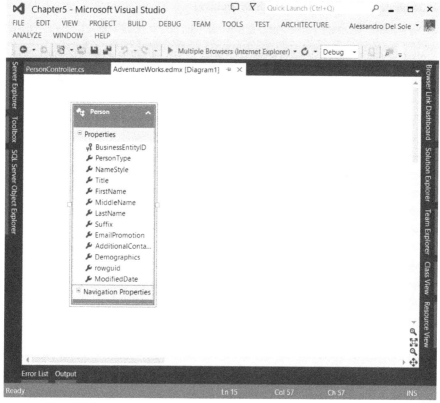

*Figure 36: The Entity Data Model designer shows the table representation.*

Depending on the database version you have installed, you might see additional entities in your designer. In fact, there are some differences between versions 2008 and 2012. You can ignore those additional entities and focus on entities you see in Figure 36. In the designer, right-click the **Demographics** property and select **Delete from Model**. The reason for this is that the **Demographics** property contains long XML markup that would make it difficult to provide readable figures for this e-book. Now that you have a connection to your data source, you need to present data and give users an opportunity of editing data. So, let's dive into scaffolding.

## Generate data-bound pages with scaffolding

The benefit of scaffolding is the ability to generate data-bound views without writing a single line of code. Visual Studio 2013 generates a controller for each entity set and one page per action, which means one page for listing a collection of items, one for adding an item, one for editing, and one for deleting. Since scaffolding generates views, in **Solution Explorer** right-click the **Views** folder, then select **Add**, **New Scaffolded Item**. The **Add Scaffold** dialog appears and allows specifying the item you need, as you can see in Figure 37.

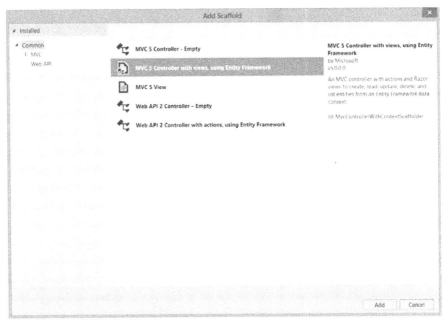

*Figure 37: Selecting an Appropriate Controller for Scaffolding*

As you can see, you can choose among different kinds of controllers. In this case you are working with the Entity Framework, so the appropriate controller is MVC 5 Controller with views, using Entity Framework. You can also choose an empty controller or a view. Also notice how you can take advantage of the Web API framework to create controllers that can be exposed to other consumers. When you click Add, Visual Studio shows the Add Controller dialog (see Figure 38).

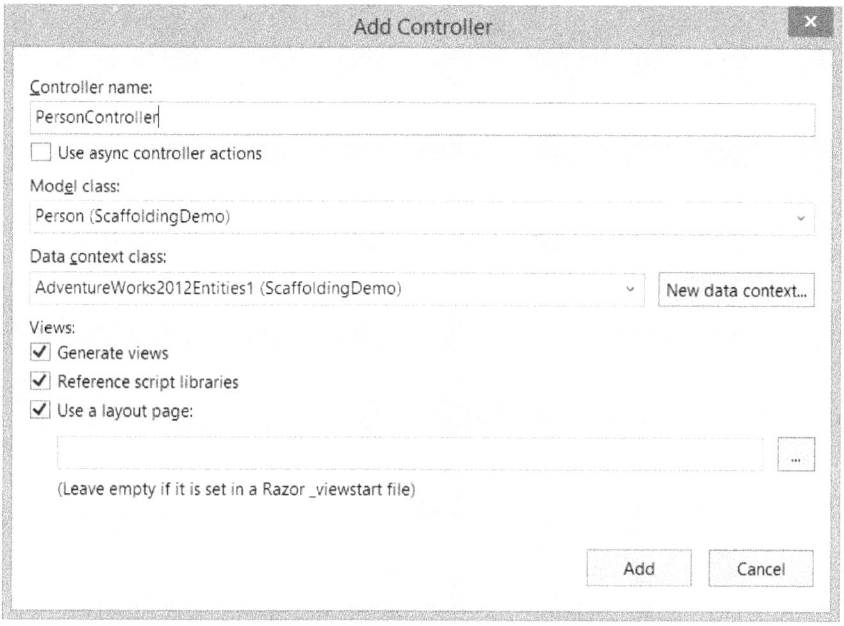

*Figure 38: Specifying Properties and Settings for the New Controller*

Here you can specify a number of settings for the new controller. The following table describes these settings and indicates how to rename items.

*Table 1: Members and settings for the Add Controller dialog*

| Item name | Description | Value |
|---|---|---|
| Controller name | The name of the controller class that will be generated to interact with data | PersonController |
| Model class | The entity class that will be managed by the controller | Person |

| Item name | Description | Value |
|---|---|---|
| Data Context class | The context class generated by the Entity Framework to represent the database in a modeled way | AdventureWorks2012Entities |
| Generate views | Select this checkbox to make Visual Studio generate views (pages) for you | True |
| Reference script libraries | Select this checkbox to import scripting libraries | True |
| Use a layout page | Select this checkbox if you want to use a custom page for the layout; no need for this example | False |

Click **Add**. In a few seconds, Visual Studio 2013 generates the `PersonController` class and a number of .cshtml files (under the Views\Person subfolder); each file is a page whose name is self-explanatory, such as Create.cshtml or Delete.cshtml. If you double-click the `PersonController` class in Solution Explorer, you will see the code that interacts with the data model. Figure 39 shows the result of scaffolding that is the controller and generated files in Solution Explorer.

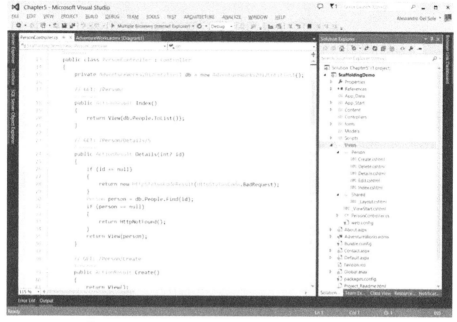

*Figure 39: The Result of Scaffolding in Solution Explorer*

The full code for the **PersonController** class follows.

*Visual C#*

```csharp
public class PersonController : Controller
{
    private AdventureWorks2012Entities1 db = new
AdventureWorks2012Entities1();

    // GET: /Person/
    public ActionResult Index()
    {
        return View(db.People.ToList());
    }

    // GET: /Person/Details/5
    public ActionResult Details(int? id)
    {
        if (id == null)
        {
            return new HttpStatusCodeResult(HttpStatusCode.BadRequest);
```

```csharp
            }
            Person person = db.People.Find(id);
            if (person == null)
            {
                return HttpNotFound();
            }
            return View(person);
        }

        // GET: /Person/Create
        public ActionResult Create()
        {
            return View();
        }

        // POST: /Person/Create
        // To protect from overposting attacks, please enable the specific
properties you want to bind to, for
        // more details see http://go.microsoft.com/fwlink/?LinkId=317598.
        [HttpPost]
        [ValidateAntiForgeryToken]
        public ActionResult
Create([Bind(Include="BusinessEntityID,PersonType,NameStyle,Title,FirstName
,MiddleName,LastName,Suffix,EmailPromotion,AdditionalContactInfo,rowguid,Mo
difiedDate")] Person person)
        {
            if (ModelState.IsValid)
            {
                db.People.Add(person);
                db.SaveChanges();
                return RedirectToAction("Index");
            }

            return View(person);
        }

        // GET: /Person/Edit/5
        public ActionResult Edit(int? id)
        {
            if (id == null)
            {
                return new HttpStatusCodeResult(HttpStatusCode.BadRequest);
            }
            Person person = db.People.Find(id);
            if (person == null)
            {
                return HttpNotFound();
            }
            return View(person);
        }
```

```csharp
        // POST: /Person/Edit/5
        // To protect from overposting attacks, please enable the specific
properties you want to bind to, for
        // more details see http://go.microsoft.com/fwlink/?LinkId=317598.
        [HttpPost]
        [ValidateAntiForgeryToken]
        public ActionResult
Edit([Bind(Include="BusinessEntityID,PersonType,NameStyle,Title,FirstName,M
iddleName,LastName,Suffix,EmailPromotion,AdditionalContactInfo,rowguid,Modi
fiedDate")] Person person)
        {
            if (ModelState.IsValid)
            {
                db.Entry(person).State = EntityState.Modified;
                db.SaveChanges();
                return RedirectToAction("Index");
            }
            return View(person);
        }

        // GET: /Person/Delete/5
        public ActionResult Delete(int? id)
        {
            if (id == null)
            {
                return new HttpStatusCodeResult(HttpStatusCode.BadRequest);
            }
            Person person = db.People.Find(id);
            if (person == null)
            {
                return HttpNotFound();
            }
            return View(person);
        }

        // POST: /Person/Delete/5
        [HttpPost, ActionName("Delete")]
        [ValidateAntiForgeryToken]
        public ActionResult DeleteConfirmed(int id)
        {
            Person person = db.People.Find(id);
            db.People.Remove(person);
            db.SaveChanges();
            return RedirectToAction("Index");
        }

        protected override void Dispose(bool disposing)
        {
            if (disposing)
```

```
            {
                db.Dispose();
            }
            base.Dispose(disposing);
        }
    }
```

*Visual Basic*

```vb
Imports System
Imports System.Collections.Generic
Imports System.Data
Imports System.Data.Entity
Imports System.Linq
Imports System.Net
Imports System.Web
Imports System.Web.Mvc

Namespace ScaffoldingDemo
    Public Class PersonController
        Inherits System.Web.Mvc.Controller

        Private db As New AdventureWorks2012Entities

        ' GET: /Person/
        Function Index() As ActionResult
            Return View(db.People.ToList())
        End Function

        ' GET: /Person/Details/5
        Function Details(ByVal id As Integer?) As ActionResult
            If IsNothing(id) Then
                Return New HttpStatusCodeResult(HttpStatusCode.BadRequest)
            End If
            Dim person As Person = db.People.Find(id)
            If IsNothing(person) Then
                Return HttpNotFound()
            End If
            Return View(person)
        End Function

        ' GET: /Person/Create
        Function Create() As ActionResult
            Return View()
        End Function

        ' POST: /Person/Create
```

```vbnet
        'To protect from overposting attacks, please enable the specific
properties you want to bind to, for
        'more details see http://go.microsoft.com/fwlink/?LinkId=317598.
        <HttpPost()>
        <ValidateAntiForgeryToken()>
        Function Create(<Bind(Include :=
"BusinessEntityID,PersonType,NameStyle,Title,FirstName,MiddleName,LastName,
Suffix,EmailPromotion,AdditionalContactInfo,rowguid,ModifiedDate")> ByVal
person As Person) As ActionResult
            If ModelState.IsValid Then
                db.People.Add(person)
                db.SaveChanges()
                Return RedirectToAction("Index")
            End If
            Return View(person)
        End Function

        ' GET: /Person/Edit/5
        Function Edit(ByVal id As Integer?) As ActionResult
            If IsNothing(id) Then
                Return New HttpStatusCodeResult(HttpStatusCode.BadRequest)
            End If
            Dim person As Person = db.People.Find(id)
            If IsNothing(person) Then
                Return HttpNotFound()
            End If
            Return View(person)
        End Function

        ' POST: /Person/Edit/5
        'To protect from overposting attacks, please enable the specific
properties you want to bind to, for
        'more details see http://go.microsoft.com/fwlink/?LinkId=317598.
        <HttpPost()>
        <ValidateAntiForgeryToken()>
        Function Edit(<Bind(Include :=
"BusinessEntityID,PersonType,NameStyle,Title,FirstName,MiddleName,LastName,
Suffix,EmailPromotion,AdditionalContactInfo,rowguid,ModifiedDate")> ByVal
person As Person) As ActionResult
            If ModelState.IsValid Then
                db.Entry(person).State = EntityState.Modified
                db.SaveChanges()
                Return RedirectToAction("Index")
            End If
            Return View(person)
        End Function

        ' GET: /Person/Delete/5
        Function Delete(ByVal id As Integer?) As ActionResult
            If IsNothing(id) Then
```

```vbnet
            Return New HttpStatusCodeResult(HttpStatusCode.BadRequest)
        End If
        Dim person As Person = db.People.Find(id)
        If IsNothing(person) Then
            Return HttpNotFound()
        End If
        Return View(person)
    End Function

    ' POST: /Person/Delete/5
    <HttpPost()>
    <ActionName("Delete")>
    <ValidateAntiForgeryToken()>
    Function DeleteConfirmed(ByVal id As Integer) As ActionResult
        Dim person As Person = db.People.Find(id)
        db.People.Remove(person)
        db.SaveChanges()
        Return RedirectToAction("Index")
    End Function

    Protected Overrides Sub Dispose(ByVal disposing As Boolean)
        If (disposing) Then
            db.Dispose()
        End If
        MyBase.Dispose(disposing)
    End Sub
End Class
End Namespace
```

Although lengthy, the code is not difficult; you have a number of methods responsible for C.R.U.D. operations, such as **Create**, **Edit**, **Details**, **Delete**, and **Index**. The latter returns the full list of records in the table mapped by the model class. Every method returns an object of type **ActionResult**, which is exposed by the MVC framework (remember you are using Web Forms here). It encapsulates the result of the aforementioned methods and is used to perform framework-level operations on behalf of the method. Of course, you can make additional edits to the controller class if you wish. In this particular example, it is a good idea to restrict the number of people returned by the **Index** method, in order to speed up the process. Imagine you want to retrieve only the first ten people in the table. You can edit the **Index** method as follows:

*Visual C#*

```csharp
// GET: /Person/
public ActionResult Index()
{
    return View(db.People.Take(10).ToList());
}
```

*Visual Basic*

```
' GET: /Person/
Function Index() As ActionResult
    Return View(db.People.Take(10).ToList())
End Function
```

You can use any LINQ operator to edit the query in a way that best fits your needs. In this case, the code uses **Take** to retrieve the first 10 records. It is worth mentioning that for each method in the code you will find some comments that explain how to invoke the related page in the browser. For instance, if you want to view the list of records in the table, you will use the /Person relative URL (see the code in the previous listing). You will get a demonstration shortly.

## Test the application

Press **F5** to start debugging the application. Your default web browser will open and show the default page of the application. In the address bar, type the /Person relative URL at the end (see the highlight in Figure 40). The application will show the first ten people in the table at this point, as you can see in Figure 40.

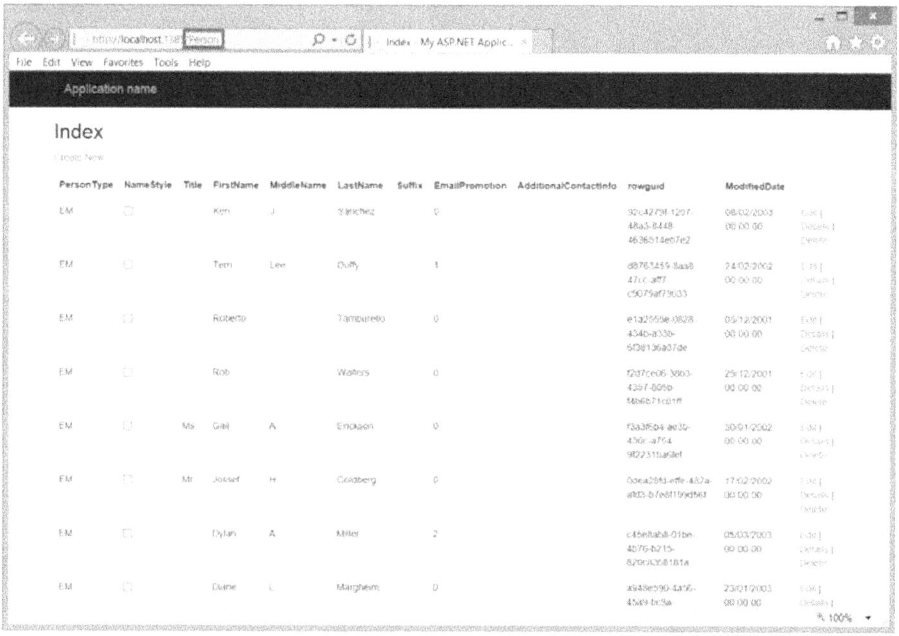

*Figure 40: The application shows a list of items.*

Notice the shortcuts to pages for data operations. For example, you can click **Edit** to see and change details of an item. This is also useful to understand how the application invokes the appropriate methods in the controller. Take a look at Figure 41, which shows how to edit an existing item.

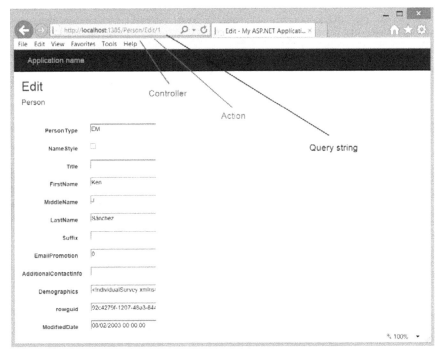

*Figure 41: Editing an Item and the Anatomy of the Address*

Apart from seeing how easy it is to edit an item without writing any code, notice look at the address bar. The address is made of the following elements:

- The web address for the application
- The name of the controller (in this case Person)
- The name of the method in the controller (in this case Edit)
- The value for the query string that will be used by the invoked method to retrieve a specific item

You can go back to the previous page and select **Create New** to see how easy it is to add a new person to the database (see Figure 42).

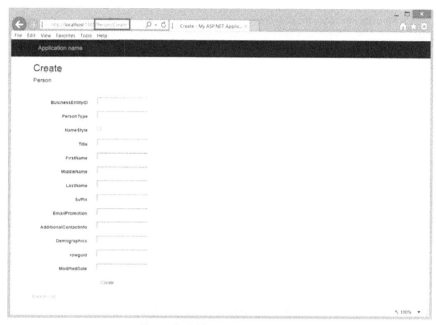

*Figure 42: Adding a New Item*

Figure 42 also highlights how both the controller name and the method name are used in the address. So you have seen how to take advantage of scaffolding in a Web Forms application due to the new One ASP.NET experience. Pages generated by Visual Studio can be edited to provide a different layout, but it is evident how with a minimal effort you can create powerful data-centric applications.

## Browsers Link Dashboard

You already know that with Visual Studio you can test your web applications with different browsers. In Visual Studio 2013, if you have your application running in different browsers and you make changes in the IDE, such changes can be refreshed to every browser with a single click. This is possible because Visual Studio 2013 and the .NET Framework 4.5.1 use SignalR 2.0, the popular library that allows sending real-time notifications.

To understand how it works, first create a new ASP.NET project called BrowserLinkDemo. By following the lesson learned in the previous section, select the **Web Forms** template and the anonymous authentication. Of course, this feature works not only with Web Forms, but also with ASP.NET MVC.

*Note: Do not delete the new project until you complete this chapter. It will be used again later when discussing the new tools for Windows Azure.*

The next step is telling Visual Studio to use multiple browsers to run the application, so if you did not do this before, select the arrow near the Start button on the toolbar (see Figure 43), then **Browse With**.

*Figure 43: Accessing the Command to Change the Default Browser(s) for Testing*

In the Browse With dialog, select two or more web browsers. On my machine, I have Internet Explorer and FireFox installed, so my selection includes both (see Figure 44).

*Figure 44: Selecting Two or More Web Browsers for Testing*

Press **CTRL** and click on each browser you want to use, then select **Set as Default** and close the dialog. Now, instead of debugging the usual way with F5, press **CTRL + F5** to start without debugging. This way, the application will be launched in all of the browsers you selected. Figure 45 shows the application running inside Internet Explorer.

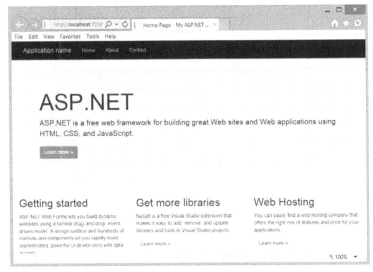

*Figure 45: The Sample Application Running*

Now let's make a very simple edit in Visual Studio. Open the Default.aspx page in the designer and replace the ASP.NET string with **Visual Studio 2013 Succinctly**. On the **Standard** toolbar, click the **Refresh** button, which you can see highlighted in Figure 46, or press **CTRL+ALT+Enter**.

*Figure 46: The Refresh Button for Linked Browsers*

Now switch back to both browsers; you will see how they show the updated string. With this technique, you do not need to stop the application, make your edits, and restart debugging. By clicking the arrow near the Refresh button, you can access additional shortcuts, including the one to enable the Browser Link Dashboard tool window. With the Browser Link Dashboard you can see connections for each application in the solution and you can take specific action for each linked browser, such as refreshing only one instead. Figure 47 shows what the Browser Link Dashboard looks like against a solution containing both sample projects described in this chapter.

*Figure 47: The Browser Link Dashboard allows managing actions for single connections.*

With Scaffolding and Browsers Link, you have seen two relevant features in Visual Studio 2013. But this new release has a great focus on the cloud. This is discussed in the next section.

# What's new in Windows Azure

Windows Azure is the popular cloud computing platform from Microsoft, first unveiled at the Professional Developer Conference (PDC) in 2008. Over the years, Windows Azure has dramatically evolved by introducing tons of services, and the cloud has become an important part of our daily lives. Many websites, mobile devices, and applications use Windows Azure's services. If you've ever developed applications for Windows Azure before, you know that you had to do most things outside of Visual Studio, using the Windows Azure Developer Portal on the web or special client applications; in fact, Visual Studio lacked a good integration with the platform. As for other platforms, Visual Studio 2013 solves the problem and provides deep integration with Windows Azure making it easy to manage many services from within the IDE. This chapter provides guidance on how Visual Studio 2013 integrates with Azure and on how you can leverage this integration to build applications faster.

## What you need before reading this section

Because we focus on the new tooling in Visual Studio 2013 for Windows Azure, we assume you already have at least a basic knowledge of the platform, including information about paid services and pricing. In fact, this chapter can neither summarize all services offered by Windows Azure nor it can explain programming for Azure, since this would require an entire book. If you need an overview of programming for Windows Azure before reading this chapter, refer to the official documentation available at http://www.windowsazure.com/en-us/documentation/ . In order to complete the steps described in this chapter, you must install the Windows Azure SDK 2.2 or later.

 *Note: This chapter describes Windows Azure from the developer's perspective and will describe services that you can access only if you have a current subscription. But Windows Azure is a paid service. Fortunately, you can enable a 30-day trial at http://www.windowsazure.com/en-us/pricing/free-trial/. If you want to fully understand the rest of this chapter, you are encouraged to subscribe the trial.*

## Server Explorer window

You've probably already used the Server Explorer tool window in Visual Studio many times, for different purposes such as managing connections to databases, or web servers. In Visual Studio 2013, Server Explorer offers a new node called Windows Azure, which allows connecting to your subscription and managing services from within the IDE. Figure 48 shows how the Windows Azure node looks.

*Figure 48: The New Windows Azure Tooling in the Server Explorer Window*

As you can see, you can manage most services without leaving Visual Studio. The first thing you need to do is associate a valid Windows Azure subscription to Visual Studio 2013. To do so, right-click **Windows Azure** and select **Connect to Windows Azure**. You will be asked to enter the Microsoft Account of your current subscription. If you have multiple subscriptions associated with your Microsoft Account, you will be able to manage subscriptions. Simply right-click again **Windows Azure** and select **Manage Subscriptions**. At this point, the Manage Windows Azure Subscriptions appears, as shown in Figure 49.

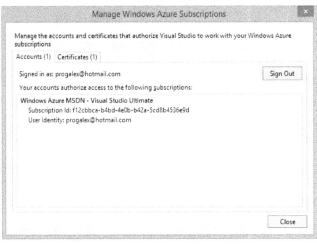

*Figure 49: Managing Windows Azure Subscriptions*

You will need to import your subscription settings in Visual Studio 2013 at this point. Click **Certificates**, then **Import**. In the appearing Import Windows Azure Subscriptions dialog (see Figure 50), click the **Download subscription file** hyperlink.

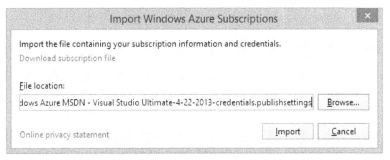

*Figure 50: Managing Windows Azure Subscriptions*

At this point, a page in the Windows Azure's website will be opened and a file with your subscription's settings will be automatically available for downloading. Once you've downloaded the settings file, click **Browse** and in the dialog search for the downloaded settings file, select it, and finally click **Import**. By following these steps, your subscription will be added to the list of subscriptions in Visual Studio. If you have added multiple subscriptions, in the Manage Windows Azure Subscriptions dialog you will be able to select the subscription you want to work with. Click **Close** when you have made your selection. Let's now see in more detail what you can do with Server Explorer.

## Integration with mobile services

Mobile Services can be used as a backend for mobile applications. A very common use of Mobile Services is storing data inside tables. In Visual Studio 2013 you can now create a mobile service directly, add tables, and see logs for the service. To create a new service, right-click **Mobile Services**, and then select **Create Service**. In the Create Mobile Service dialog you will have to specify the new service's details, as shown in Figure 51.

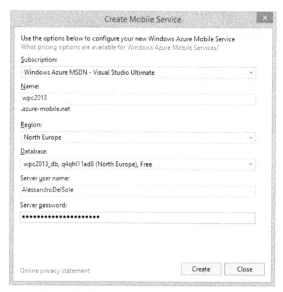

*Figure 51: Creating a New Mobile Service*

You will need to specify the following information:

- The subscription where the service will be created. You can leave the selection unchanged if you want the service to be created in the current subscription.
- The service name. Visual Studio 2013 will check the availability of the service name as you type.
- The Region. Remember to select the region that is nearest to your location.
- A new or existing SQL Azure database to be associated with the new service (optional). If you did not create a SQL Azure database in the Management Portal before, you can use the **Create a free SQL database** option or the **Create a billed SQL database**. Of course, I strongly recommend to create a free SQL Azure database (up to 20 MB) rather than a billed one.
- User name and password for the SQL Azure server in order to access the database.

 *Note: I'm assuming you have already configured a SQL Azure server, since I'm talking about server user name and password required to access a database on the cloud. If you*

*did not configure your SQL Azure server, you can get started by reading the official documentation.*

When you're finished, click **Create**. The new service will appear under the Mobile Services node of Server Explorer. You can also add tables to the service directly. Right-click the service's name and select **Create Table**. In the Create Table dialog (see Figure 52) you can specify the table name and permission for each of the C.R.U.D. operations.

*Figure 52: Creating a New Mobile Service*

Now create a new table called **TodoItem**. We will use this table in the next chapter when demonstrating Windows 8 support for mobile services. Notice how you have deep control over permissions; you can allow everyone, authenticated users, administrators, or users having the application key (managing the application key is only available in the management portal). Click **Create** when you're ready. You will be able to see the new table as a node under the mobile service's name. Also, if you expand the table name, you will see a number of JavaScript code files, which are responsible of performing operations against data, such as read, insert, update, and delete. Figure 53 shows how the Server Explorer window appears at this point.

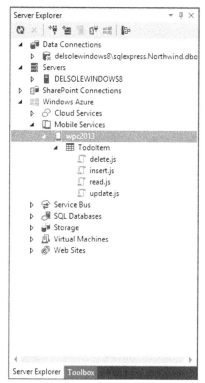

*Figure 53: Mobile service, table, and JavaScript files as they appear in Server Explorer.*

With only a few steps, you have created a mobile service that can be used as a backend in your mobile applications. You can use mobile services in the following applications:

- Windows Store apps for Windows 8.x
- Windows Phone apps
- ASP.NET web applications

You will need to right-click the project name in Solution Explorer and select **Add Connected Service**. This is discussed further in Chapter 7.

### Integration with Azure websites and cloud services

In Windows Azure, you publish your web applications through websites or cloud services. A website is a simplified, pre-configured environment for easy deployment. A cloud service, instead, is a highly customizable environment that requires you to make some configurations before deployment, and where you can take a lot of actions over the system. You can find the full description of both environments in this page of the Windows Azure documentation (I recommend that you read it). Whatever your choice is, Visual Studio 2013 supports publishing applications to both web sites and cloud services.

 *Note: You can connect to Virtual Machines from Server Explorer, but you can only publish to websites and cloud services directly.*

For instance, imagine you want to deploy the sample application created earlier in this chapter to demonstrate the Browser Link feature. In Server Explorer, right-click the **Web Sites** node and then select **Add New Site**. A new dialog called Create site on Windows Azure appears. Here you will have to specify details for the new website, as shown in Figure 54.

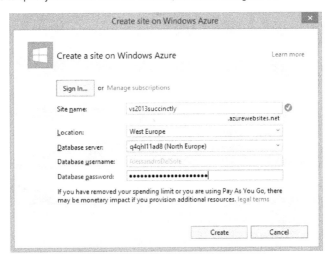

*Figure 54: Creating a New Website*

The following information is required:

- The site name, an identifier that will be used to construct the website's URL. Visual Studio will check for the availability of the name as you type.
- The location: Microsoft has several data centers across the world, so ensure you select the location nearest to you.
- Database server, database username, and database password. These are optional fields; you only need to supply them if your application will use an SQL Azure database.

*Tip: The sample application does not use any database. For the sake of completeness, Figure 54 shows how to fill database-related fields.*

Once you have entered all the required information, click **Create**. Once the website has been created, double-click its name in Server Explorer so that Visual Studio shows a configuration window (see Figure 55).

*Figure 55: Configuration Window for the New Website*

The window is divided into four main areas:

- Actions: here you find shortcuts to common tasks such as opening the site in the Azure's management portal, stopping or restarting the site.
- Web Site Settings: here you can fine-tune the configuration for your website, including error management and tracing.
- Connection Strings: here you can manage connection strings that your application uses to connect to data sources.
- Application Settings: this allows listing and adding environment variables for your websites. You should never change or remove settings added by Visual Studio.

Now you want to publish the BrowserLinkDemo sample application to the newly created website. First, right-click the project name in Solution Explorer, then select Convert, Convert to

Windows Azure Cloud Service Project. This action will add a new project with a Windows Azure role to the solution. By default, the new project's name has the same name of the original project plus the .Azure suffix, in our example it is BrowserLinkDemo.Azure. Now, in Solution Explorer right-click the original project (BrowserLinkDemo) and then click Publish.

 *Tip: Use the Publish command if you want to deploy your application to a website. Because this is our current case, we are using this option. If you want to deploy to a Cloud Service instead, right-click the project name and select Publish to Windows Azure. A specific dialog will allow creating a new Cloud Service and easily deploy the application.*

The Publish Web dialog appears and has no preconfigured settings, so you need to click the **Import** button to specify the target website. Visual Studio shows the Import Publish Settings dialog at this point, which is visible in Figure 55.

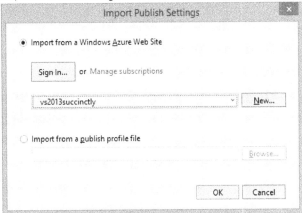

*Figure 56: Selecting the Website for Publishing*

Since the IDE is still connected to your Azure subscription, you can simply select the target website from the first combo box. You can also select a different subscription by clicking **Sign In** or by importing an existing publish profile file.

 *Tip: Visual Studio 2013 makes it easy to download and publish profiles from your Windows Azure subscription. Just right-click a website in Server Explorer and then click Download Publish Profile.*

When you're ready, click **OK**. The Profile form in the Publish Web dialog will be filled with information coming from the publish profile you just selected. Go ahead to the **Connection** form (see Figure 57).

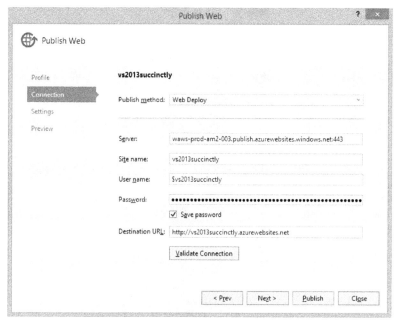

*Figure 57: Connection Settings for the Application*

Visual Studio 2013 automatically provides information for this form so you do not need to change any field. Notice the content of the Destination URL field, which contains the web address for your application once published. Click **Next** to access the Settings form (see Figure 58).

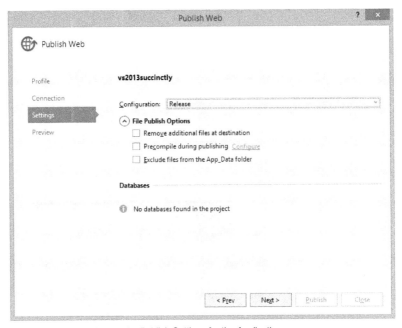

*Figure 58: Publish Settings for the Application*

In this form of the Publish Web dialog you can change the configuration between **Release** (default) and **Debug**, or decide if you want to remove additional files at destination, precompile managed code during publishing, or exclude files from the App_Data folder. If you are also using a database, here you will be able to set a default connection string. When you click **Next**, you access the Preview form where you can optionally view the full list of files that will be published to the websites, by clicking **Start Preview**. The result of pressing this button is shown in Figure 59.

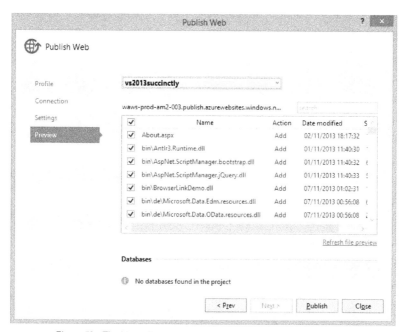

*Figure 59: The List of Files that Will Be Published to the Website*

You can finally click **Publish**. The progress of publishing will be shown in the Output window and the speed may vary depending on your Internet connection. When the application has been published and is online, you will see a message in the Output window and you will be able to start the application by using the appropriate web address. Figure 60 shows the sample application running on the website created previously.

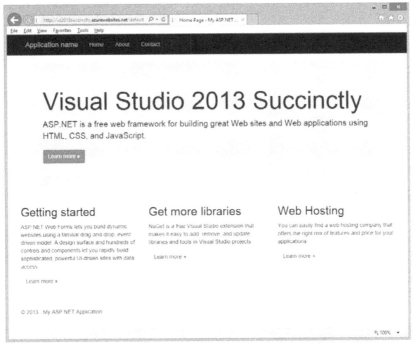

*Figure 60: The Sample Application Running on the Website*

As you can see, with a very few steps you have been able to publish an ASP.NET application to Windows Azure, without the need of having an in-house server and hosting infrastructure.

 *Note: If you create websites for testing purposes like in the current scenario, remember to delete the site when finished, even if you have the spending limit enabled. Websites consume resources even if they are offline, so the only way to ensure they do not consume any unneeded resources to delete them.*

## Integration with Azure Storage

 *Note: For the rest of Azure services described in this chapter, we focus on the new tools in the IDE. If you need guidance on how to access resources in the Azure Storage from your applications, make sure you read the appropriate documentation.*

The Windows Azure Storage is the place where you can store data and files for your cloud-based applications. For instance, if your application needs to show some pictures or allows downloading files, these will be first saved onto the Storage and then accessed via their web address (HTTP). The Windows Azure Storage provides the following services:

- Blob Storage: here you can upload unstructured binary data, such as files.

- Queue Storage: this is used to save and retrieve messages for workflows and communications.
- Table Storage: here you can store non-relational and unschematized data with support for queries.

The Blob Storage can also recognize VHD files and allows mounting these files as virtual hard disks on the cloud. Visual Studio 2013 finally provides integration with the Windows Azure Storage from within the IDE. This is a tremendous benefit and a significant step forward, because before Visual Studio 2013, the only way to upload to or manage information on the Storage was by using 3rd party client applications. Now you can definitely use Visual Studio to perform operations such as uploading files to the Blob Storage. Any Windows Azure subscription supports multiple storages. For each storage, you need to create a storage account. Since any transaction (download, upload, login) has a cost, Microsoft offers the Development Account, which consists of the Windows Azure Emulator and other components that allow simulating a production environment on your development machine. This way, you can freely test transactions locally, and move to the cloud only when you are ready to go to production. Remember to check the MSDN documentation for the storage programmability and for understanding how to access information on the storage from your applications.

### Creating a storage account

In Server Explorer, expand the **Storage** node under Windows Azure. The local development storage will be shown by default. If it's not already running, Visual Studio will start the Windows Azure Storage Emulator. The development storage works exactly like an online storage; however, it is a good idea to see how to work with an online account. Unfortunately, you cannot create new storage accounts from Visual Studio; instead, you can connect to existing accounts. So, open the Windows Azure Management Portal in your favorite web browser. Once logged in, click **Storage** in the dashboard on the left. Figure 61 shows how the management portal appears at this point, with no accounts available yet.

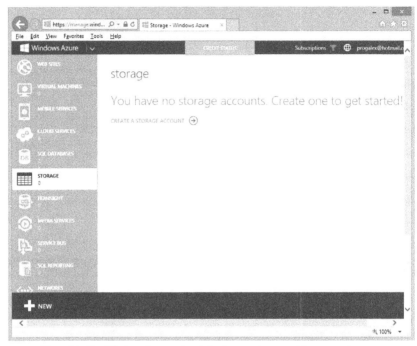

*Figure 61: The Windows Azure subscription has no storages at the moment.*

Click **CREATE A STORAGE ACCOUNT**. The Management Portal will open a new page where you can easily create a new storage account by supplying the account name and the location. Figure 62 shows how the management portal appears at this point.

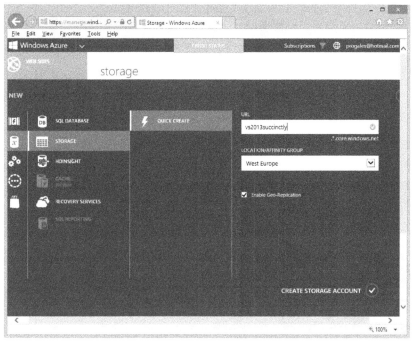

*Figure 62: Creating a New Storage Account*

Always remember to select the nearest location to where you live. As you might know, the account name becomes the prefix of the URL for services exposed by the storage. Table 2 shows URLs for each service (where storagename is the name you entered when creating the storage account).

*Table 2: Members and settings for the Add Controller dialog*

| Storage | URL |
| --- | --- |
| Blob Storage | http://storagename.blob.core.windows.net |
| Table Storage | http://storagename.table.core.windows.net |
| Queue Storage | http://storagename.queue.core.windows.net |

Addresses shown in Table 2 are very important, since they are the way you access each storage. Click **CREATE STORAGE ACCOUNT**. After about one minute, you will be able to see the storage account online in the Management Portal. Now close the management portal and go back to Visual Studio 2013. In Server Explorer, right-click the **Storage** node and then click **Refresh**. You will now see the newly created storage account (see Figure 63).

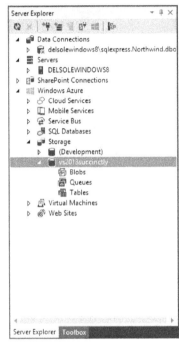

*Figure 63: The new Storage Account is visible inside Server Explorer.*

Now you will see how to interact with the storage.

## Managing the Blob Storage

Say you want to upload an image file to the Blob Storage. Blobs are organized within folders called containers, so you first need to create a container. Follow these steps:

1. Click the Storage Account of your interest (in this case, vs2013succinctly) and expand it in order to make the Blobs node visible.
2. Select **Create Blob Container**.
3. In the Create Blob Container dialog (see Figure 64), specify the name of your new container all lower case. For example, enter **pictures**.
4. The new container will be visible in Server Explorer. Right-click it and select **View Blob Container**. You will see a new window called Container whose purpose is showing and

filtering the list of blobs in a container. It also allows uploading and/or deleting blobs (see Figure 65).

5. Click the **Upload Blob** button (the one with the black arrow). In the file selection dialog, select an image file (possibly of type Jpeg, in order to save space and time due to the lower size of this format). Visual Studio will start uploading your file to the storage, showing the progress of the operation. As you can see from Figure 66, the window shows metadata information for the file and, most importantly, the URL to access it.

*Figure 64: Creating a New Blob Container*

*Figure 65: The list of blobs for the current container is empty.*

*Figure 66: The blob has been uploaded and you can see its metadata and URL.*

If you right-click the blob, you will get a popup menu showing a list of interesting commands. You can download the blob to disk (Save As), open the blob (Open), delete the blob (Delete), view more detailed properties in the Properties window (Properties), and copy the blob's URL to the clipboard (Copy URL). In order to access the blob in code, you will need to supply a connection string and credentials for your Windows Azure subscription. Writing code to accomplish this is beyond the scope of this chapter, so read this page in the Windows Azure documentation for this purpose. What you really need to understand is how you can upload the blob (and how you can manage blobs and containers) with the new tooling in Visual Studio 2013, without the need of 3rd party client applications.

## Create and query tables

The Windows Azure storage supports creating tables to store nonrelational data. Right-click **Tables** in your storage account and select **Create Table**. In the **Create Table** dialog (see Figure 67), enter the name of your table, for example **mydata**.

*Figure 67: Creating a New Table*

When the new table is created, double-click it: you will see a window similar to the one you saw for containers. The window's toolbar (see Figure 68) has a button called Add Entity, represented by three drawers and a green addition symbol.

*Figure 68: The Table's Designer Toolbar*

Click **Add Entity** to enter new data. Figure 69 shows how you can enter data for the new entity.

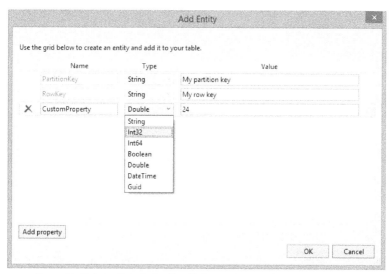

*Figure 69: Entering Data for the New Entity and Property Customization*

Every entity has some predefined properties, such as PartitionKey and RowKey, both of type String, that can be assigned with your values. Also, you can add custom properties of different types (see Figure 69). Click **OK** when ready. The new entity will be now visible inside the window, as shown in Figure 70.

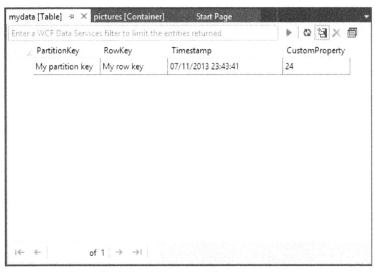

*Figure 70: Listing Tables in your Storage Account*

The toolbar has another button called Query Builder (the one on the right represented by two overlaid squares as shown in Figure 68), which allows executing queries against tables. You can specify one or more filters against different properties, as shown in Figure 71.

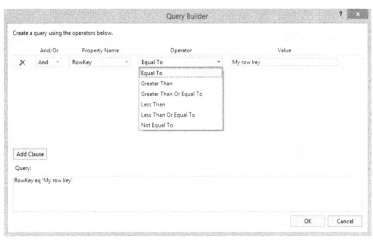

*Figure 71: Defining Queries with the Query Builder*

Notice that custom properties are not available in the Property Name dropdown. However, you can type queries and add filters by custom properties in the textbox inside the designer's toolbar (see Figure 68). When you have defined all the required filters, click **OK**. You will see the query syntax in the text box; if you click **Execute**, the query will be executed and only entities matching the specified criteria will be shown.

## Create message queues

Visual Studio 2013 supports creating queues in the storage. With queues, cloud-based applications can easily share messages. To create a queue, in Server Explorer expand **Storage**, then expand the storage account of your choice (you can use **Development**), then right-click **Queues**. In the **Create Queue** dialog, enter the name for the new queue, again lower case (see Figure 72).

*Figure 72: Creating a New Queue*

When the new queue is visible in Server Explorer, double-click it to open the Queue window. Here is the place where you add and manage messages. To add one, click **Add Message** on the toolbar (the button with the icon of a letter and the green + symbol). In the appearing **Add Message** dialog, enter a text message and define when the message will expire (see Figure 73), and then click **OK**.

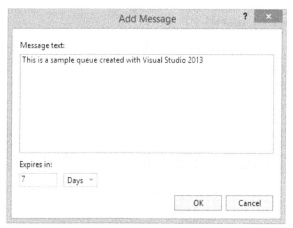

*Figure 73: Creating a New Message*

The new message will be added to the queue and will be visible in the Queue window, as you can see in Figure 74.

*Figure 74: Creating a New Queue*

Interesting information is shown, such as the insertion time, expiration time, and ID. By using the appropriate buttons on the toolbar, you can also de-queue or remove messages. If you are not familiar with using queues in your applications, check out the Windows Azure documentation about programming with queues. As for other storage types, Visual Studio 2013 makes it very easy to create and manage queues avoiding the need of using 3<sup>rd</sup> party applications.

## Chapter summary

With the idea of offering the most productive environment ever, Visual Studio 2013 introduces many new tools for web development, including building applications for Windows Azure. On the ASP.NET side, Visual Studio 2013 introduces the One ASP.NET experience, which provides a unified approach to web development making it easy to use libraries from different frameworks into one application. This includes the use of scaffolding (formerly available only for MVC applications) in Web Forms applications. With scaffolding you can easily build data-centric applications and take advantage of auto-generated code for data access and data-bound, ready-to-use pages. Also, Visual Studio 2013 makes it easier to test applications in different web browsers with the new Browser Link feature, which allows refreshing all browsers with one click. For Windows Azure, Visual Studio 2013 enhances the Server Explorer tool window, which now offers all you need to work with most services exposed by the platform from within the IDE.

# Chapter 6 New and Enhanced Tools for Debugging

As a developer, you probably spend a lot of time testing and debugging your code. Visual Studio 2013 introduces new debugging tools and updates some existing ones, continuing in its purpose of offering the most productive environment ever.

## 64-bit Edit and Continue

Visual Studio 2013 finally introduces Edit and Continue for 64-bit applications. As you know, with Edit and Continue, you can break the application's execution, edit your code, and then restart. So far, this has been available only for 32-bit applications. It is very easy to demonstrate how this feature works. Consider a very simple Console application, whose goal is retrieving the list of running processes and displaying the name of the first process in the list; the code is the following.

*Visual C#*

```csharp
class Program
{
    static void Main(string[] args)
    {
        var runningProcesses = System.Diagnostics.
                            Process.GetProcesses();
        Console.WriteLine(runningProcesses.First().ProcessName);
        Console.ReadLine();
    }
}
```

*Visual Basic*

```vb
Module Module1

    Sub Main()
        'Add a breakpoint here and make your edits at 64-bits!
        Dim runningProcesses = System.Diagnostics.Process.GetProcesses()
        Console.WriteLine(runningProcesses.First().ProcessName)
        Console.ReadLine()
    End Sub

End Module
```

Before running the application, open the project's properties, select the **Build** tab, and change the platform target to **x64**, as shown in Figure 75.

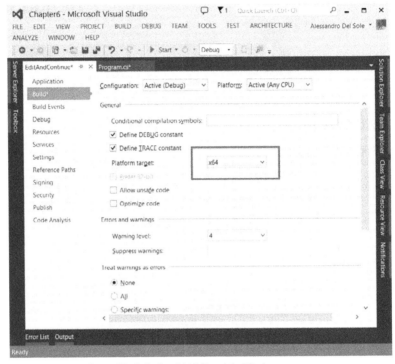

*Figure 75: Selecting 64-bit Target Architectures*

Now go back to the code, and place a breakpoint on the line containing the declaration of the `runningProcesses` variable by pressing **F9**. Finally, press **F5** to run the application. When the debugger encounters the breakpoint, the code editor is shown. You can simply rename the `runningProcesses` variable into `currentProcesses` (see Figure 76); this is enough to demonstrate how Edit and Continue is now working. Before Visual Studio 2013, if you tried to edit your code, at this point you would receive an error saying that Edit and Continue is only supported in 32-bit applications.

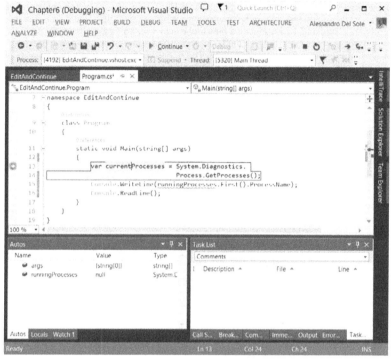

Figure 76: You can edit your code before resuming the execution.

## Asynchronous debugging

Visual Studio 2012 and the .NET Framework 4.5 introduced a new pattern for coding asynchronous operations, known as the Async/Await pattern based on the new **async** and **await** keywords in the managed languages. The goal of this pattern is making the UI thread always responsive; the compiler can generate appropriate instances of the Task class and execute an operation asynchronously even in the same thread. You will see shortly a code example that will make your understanding easier, however there is very much more to say about Async/Await, so you are strongly encouraged to read the MSDN documentation if you've never used it. I f you are already familiar with this pattern, you know that it is pretty difficult to get information about the progress and the state of an asynchronous operation at debugging time. For this reason, Visual Studio 2013 introduces a new tool window called Tasks. The purpose of this new tool window is to show the list of running tasks and provide information on active and pending tasks, time of execution, and executing code. The Tasks window has been very much publicized as a new addition to Windows Store apps development, but it is actually available to a number of other technologies, such as WPF. This is the reason why this feature is discussed in this chapter rather than in the next one about Windows 8.1.

## Create a sample project

To understand how this feature works, let's create a new WPF Application project called *AsyncDebugging*. This application will create a new text file when the user clicks a button. The XAML code for the user interface is very simple, as represented in the following listing.

```
<Window x:Class="AsyncDebugging.MainWindow"
        xmlns="http://schemas.microsoft.com/winfx/2006/xaml/presentation"
        xmlns:x="http://schemas.microsoft.com/winfx/2006/xaml"
        Title="MainWindow" Height="350" Width="525">
    <Grid>
        <Button Width="100" Height="30" Name="FileButton" Content="Create
file" Click="FileButton_Click"/>
    </Grid>
</Window>
```

The code-behind file for the main window will contain the following code (see comments inside).

*Visual C#*

```csharp
using System.IO;

        //Asynchronous method that passes some variables to
        //the other async method that will write the file
        //You wait for the async operation to be completed by using
        //the await operator. This method cannot be awaited itself
        //because it returns void.
        private async void WriteFile()
        {
            string filePath = @"C:\temp\testFile.txt";
            string text = "Visual Studio 2013 Succinctly\r\n";

            await WriteTextAsync(filePath, text);
        }


        //Asynchronous method that writes some text into a file
        //Marked with "async"
```

```csharp
private async Task WriteTextAsync(string filePath, string text)
{
    byte[] encodedText = Encoding.Unicode.GetBytes(text);

    using (FileStream sourceStream = new FileStream(filePath,
        FileMode.Append, FileAccess.Write, FileShare.None,
        bufferSize: 4096, useAsync: true))
    {
        //new APIs since .NET 4.5 offer async methods to read
        //and write files
        //you use "await" to wait for the async operation to be
        //completed and to get the result
        await sourceStream.WriteAsync(encodedText, 0,
            encodedText.Length);
    };
}

private void FileButton_Click(object sender, RoutedEventArgs e)
{
    //Place a breakpoint here...
    WriteFile();
}
```

*Visual Basic*

```vbnet
Imports System.IO

'Asynchronous method that passes some variables to
'the other async method that will write the file
'You wait for the async operation to be completed by using
'the await operator. This method cannot be awaited itself
'because it returns void.
Private Async Sub WriteFile()
    Dim filePath As String = "C:\temp\testFile.txt"
    Dim text As String = "Visual Studio 2013 Succinctly"

    Await WriteTextAsync(filePath, text)
End Sub

'Requires Imports System.IO
'Asynchronous method that writes some text into a file
'Marked with "async"
Private Async Function WriteTextAsync(filePath As String,
        text As String) As Task
    Dim encodedText As Byte() = Encoding.Unicode.GetBytes(text)

    Using sourceStream As New FileStream(filePath, FileMode.Append,
                                        FileAccess.Write,
```

```
                                              FileShare.None,
                                              bufferSize:=4096,
                                              useAsync:=True)
            'new APIs since .NET 4.5: async methods to read and write files
            'you use "await" to wait for the async operation
            'to be completed and to get the result
            Await sourceStream.WriteAsync(encodedText, 0,
                    encodedText.Length)
        End Using
    End Function

    Private Sub FileButton_Click(sender As Object, e As RoutedEventArgs)
        WriteFile()
    End Sub
```

In order to run the code without any errors, ensure you have a C:\Temp folder; if not, create one or edit the code to point to a different folder. If you start the application normally, after a few seconds you will see that the text file has been created correctly into the C:\Temp folder. If you already have used the Async/Await pattern in the past, you know that the debugging tools available until Visual Studio 2012 could not show the lifecycle of tasks; you could not know what task was active and which one was waiting. Let's see how Visual Studio 2013 changes things at this point.

## Understanding the Tasks lifecycle with the Tasks window

Place a breakpoint on the **WriteFile** method invocation inside the button's click event handler (see the comment in the previous listing). Start the application and, when ready, click the button. When Visual Studio breaks the execution on the breakpoint, go to **Debug**, **Windows**, and select **Tasks**. The Tasks tool window will be opened and docked inside the IDE. Start debugging with Step Into by pressing **F11**. While asynchronous methods are invoked, the Tasks window shows their status, as demonstrated in Figure 77.

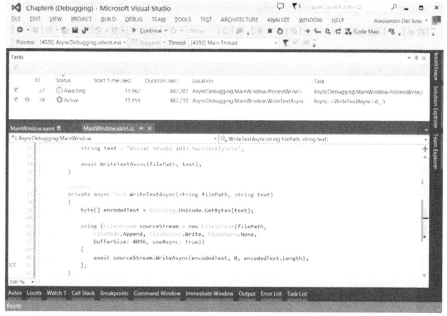

*Figure 77: The Tasks window shows the status of asynchronous tasks.*

By default, the Tasks window shows the following columns and related information:

- ID, which represents the task identifier.
- Status, which indicates whether the task is active or awaiting.
- Start Time (sec), which indicates the start time in seconds for the tasks.
- Location, which shows the name of the method where the task has been invoked.
- Task, which summarizes the operation in progress.

You can customize the Task window by adding or removing columns. If you right-click any column and then select **Columns**, a popup menu will show the full list of available columns; for instance, you might be interested in the Thread Assignment column to see what thread contains the selected task. The Tasks window is definitely useful when you need a better understanding of asynchronous operations' lifecycle, including when you need to analyze a task's performance. If the Tasks window does not display information as you step through lines of code using F11, and you are working with a desktop application, restart debugging and retry. This is a known issue. If you are working with a Windows Store app instead, you will not encounter this problem.

# Performance and Diagnostics Hub

Analyzing performance and the behavior of an application is crucial. If your application is fast, fluid, and does not consume a lot of system resources (including battery for mobile apps), users will love it. Visual Studio has been offering analysis tools for many years, focusing on different areas such as memory usage, CPU usage, unit tests, and code analysis. With the big growth of mobile apps, Visual Studio has also been offering analysis tools specific to mobile platforms. In Visual Studio 2013, Microsoft has made another step forward, introducing a new unique place where you find such analysis tools. This place is called Performance and Diagnostics Hub. You can reach it by selecting **Debug**, **Performance** and **Diagnostics** or by pressing **ALT+F2**. Figure 78 shows how the Performance and Diagnostics Hub appears with a Windows Store app project.

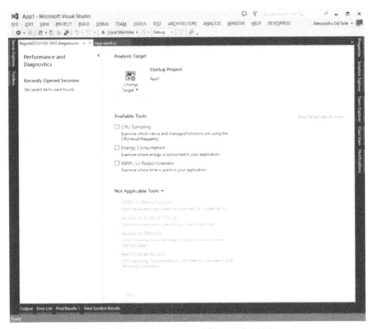

*Figure 78: The Performance and Diagnostics Hub*

Visual Studio 2013 will enable only target-specific tools. Figure 78 refers to a XAML Windows Store app, so all the other tools that target HTML Windows Store apps are disabled. For ASP.NET and desktop applications, only the CPU Sampling is available. Table 3 shows the list of available analysis tools per project type.

*Table 3: Analysis Tools per Project Type*

| Analysis Tool | Purpose | Project Type(s) |
|---|---|---|
| Performance Wizard (includes CPU Sampling) | Analyze CPU usage, managed memory allocation, runtime diagnostics of the application state | All project types |
| Energy Consumption | Analyze potential battery usage through the Windows simulator | Windows Store apps |
| XAML UI Responsiveness | Analyze how time is spent in rendering layout | XAML Windows Store apps |
| HTML UI Responsiveness | Analyze how time is spent in rendering layout | HTML Windows Store apps |
| JavaScript Memory | Analyze the JavaScript heap to help find issues such as memory leaks | HTML Windows Store apps |
| JavaScript Function Timing | Analyze how time is spent in executing JavaScript code | HTML Windows Store apps |

The CPU Sampling analysis tool invokes the Profiler that ships with Visual Studio, which you already know from previous versions. To start a diagnostics session you just select the tool you need and then click **Start** at the bottom of the page. When you close the application or break the diagnostic session manually, Visual Studio will generate a report based on the analysis type you selected. In the next chapter, when we discuss new features for Windows 8.1, you will get a more detailed demonstration of this tool. Remember that you can still access analysis tools via the Analyze menu as you did with previous versions of the IDE.

# Code Map debugging

 *Note: Code Map is available only in Visual Studio 2013 Ultimate.*

Another interesting addition to Visual Studio 2013 is Code Map. Actually, Code Map is available in Visual Studio 2012 with Update 1, but now the tool is integrated in the IDE. With Code Map, you can get an incremental visualization of your application and dependencies. In simpler words, you can get a visual representation of method calls, references, and fields while debugging, inside an interactive window where you can also add comments, flag an item for follow up, and export graphics to an image file.

To understand how Code Map works, let's consider the WPF sample application we created to demonstrate asynchronous debugging earlier in this chapter. Ensure a breakpoint is still inside the button's click event handler, then start the application with **F5**. Click the button in the application, then when the debugger encounters the breakpoint and breaks, click the **Code Map** on the toolbar (see Figure 79).

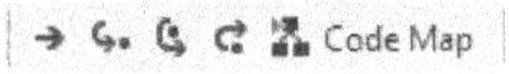

*Figure 79: The Code Map Button*

Visual Studio will start generating a map at this point. After a few seconds, you will see the method call in the Code Map, as represented in Figure 80.

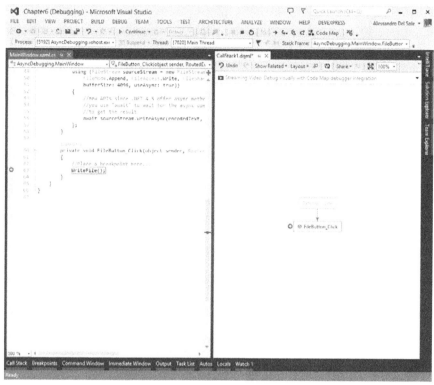

*Figure 80: A New Code Map*

Before continuing, you can play with the various buttons on the window's toolbar. For instance, if you check the Share button, you will see how you can easily export or email the diagram as an image file or as a portable XPS file. The Layout button offers an option to show the code map in different ways, whereas Show Related allows finding references to methods and types for the selected item in the map. Now press **F11** to execute the next line of code. The Code Map is immediately updated with the call to the `WriteFile` method, as shown in Figure 81.

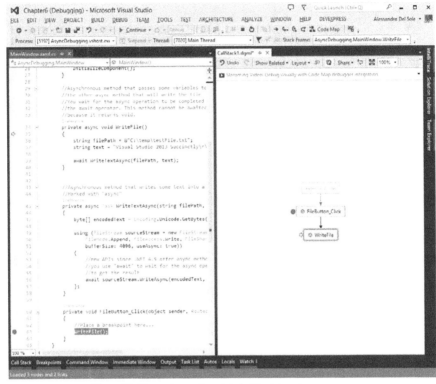

*Figure 81: The code map is updated while debugging.*

Objects are also represented on the Code Map. For example, while you are debugging the
`WriteFile` method, right-click the **text** variable and then click **Show On Code Map**. The map
will be updated (see Figure 82) with the referenced variable, shown inside its containing object.

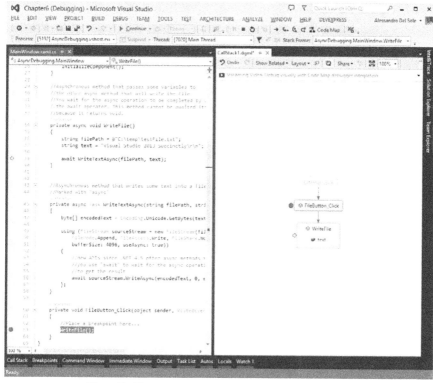

Figure 82:  The code map is updated while debugging.

If you right-click a method in the map, you will be able to display a number of data points such as calls to other methods, fields the method references, and the containing type. For example, right-click the `WriteFile` method and then select **Show Methods This Call**. Visual Studio will show calls to other methods made by `WriteFile`, as shown in Figure 83.

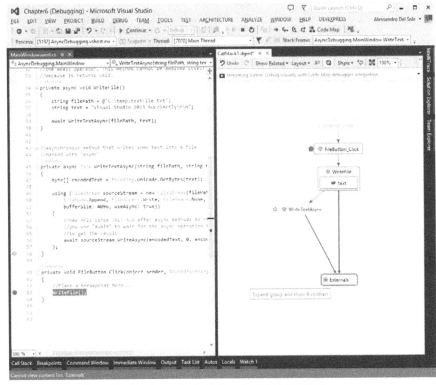

*Figure 83: Showing method calls from the selected method.*

The method calls **WriteTextAsync**, which invokes external code. Such an external code is how the runtime translates the Async/Await pattern into the backing .NET methods. This can be easily demonstrated by expanding the **Externals** node by clicking the expansion button inside. As a tooltip suggests, if you expand the Externals node you will be able to see nine children objects, as represented in Figure 84.

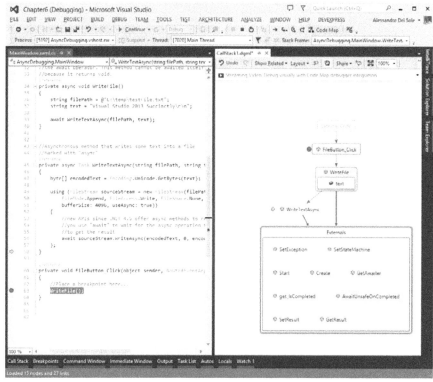

Figure 84: Investigating External Calls

All the method calls you see in the map are handled by the runtime to manage asynchronous operations on your behalf. It is worth mentioning that every time you pass the mouse pointer over a method, a tooltip shows the method definition in code. You can also add comments and flag items for follow up. To add a comment, right-click an item and then select **New Comment**. You will be able to enter your comment inside a text box. To flag an item for follow up, right-click it and then select **Flag for Follow Up**. In Figure 85, you can see a comment and the `WriteTextAsync` method flagged for follow up.

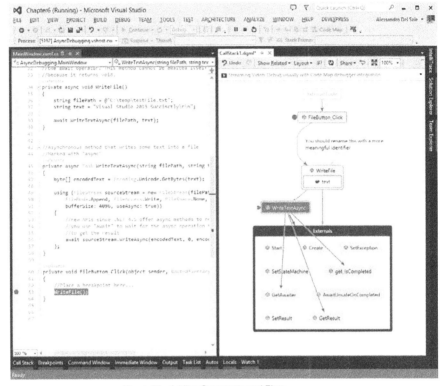

*Figure 85: Adding Comments and Flags*

You can finally right-click an item and see advanced properties by selecting the **Advanced** group in the context menu. Figure 86 shows the result of the command **Show Containing Type**, **Namespace**, and **Assembly**.

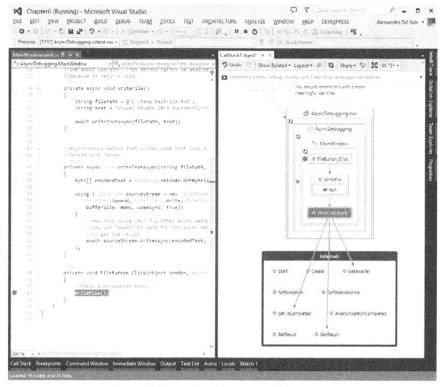

*Figure 86: Visualizing Advanced Properties*

It is worth mentioning that the context menu you see when you right-click any items will show the Go To Definition command, which will redirect you to the object definition in either the code editor or the Object Browser window. As you can easily understand, Code Map provides a great benefit because it allows debugging while literally seeing what is happening; this makes it easier to discover the most subtle bugs.

# Method Return Value

Visual Studio 2013 brings to Visual C# and Visual Basic a feature that was already available to C++, which is the ability to view a method's return value inside the Autos window without the need to step into the code. To understand how this feature works, create a new Console application. Now consider the following code.

*Visual C#*

```csharp
class Program
{
    static void Main(string[] args)
    {
        //Step Over (F10)
        int result = Multiply(Five(), Six());
    }

    private static int Multiply(int num1, int num2)
    {
        return (num1 * num2);
    }

    private static int Five()
    {
        return (5);
    }

    private static int Six()
    {
        return (6);
    }
}
```

*Visual Basic*

```vb
Module Module1

    Sub Main()
        'Step over (F10)
        Dim result As Integer = Multiply(Five(), Six())
    End Sub

    Private Function Multiply(num1 As Integer, num2 As Integer) As Integer
        Return (num1 * num2)
    End Function

    Private Function Five() As Integer
        Return (5)
    End Function

    Private Function Six() As Integer
        Return (6)
    End Function
End Module
```

As you can see, this simplified code returns the result of a multiplication by invoking two methods, each returning an integer value. As suggested in the code, place a breakpoint on the only line of code in the **Main** method and start the application by pressing **F5**. You can step over (**F10**) to execute the method without executing the other methods line by line. At this point, you will be able to see the value returned by every intermediate method call in the Autos window, as shown in Figure 87.

 *Tip: If the Autos window is not displayed automatically, go to Debug, then select Windows, then Autos.*

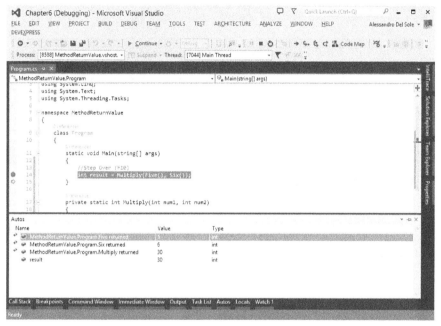

*Figure 87: Method Return Values Shown in the Autos Window Without Executing Line by Line*

This feature is useful when you need to focus on one piece of code and you do not want to step into every single line, but you still want to see the result of every method call.

## Chapter summary

Because debugging is one of the most important activities in application development, Microsoft has made a significant investment to make the debugging experience in Visual Studio 2013 even more productive. Now you can finally use the popular Edit and Continue feature against 64-bit applications. You can take advantage of asynchronous debugging to understand the lifecycle of asynchronous operations based on the Async/Await pattern. You now have a unified place to analyze your applications' performances and behavior with the new Performance and Diagnostics Hub. You can get a graphical representation of your code execution while debugging with Code Map. Finally, you can now get method return values without stepping into every single line of code, just by stepping over the caller method. All these new features will save you time and help you write high-quality code.

# Chapter 7 Visual Studio 2013 for Windows 8.1

One reason for the release of a new version of Visual Studio after only one year is that several technologies other have been updated. Probably the most important update has been Windows 8.1., which introduces many new APIs and changes in the existing infrastructure. Because of this, developers need an updated version of the .NET Framework (the 4.5.1) to support Windows 8.1 and a new version of Visual Studio based on .NET 4.5.1. This chapter covers new features in the IDE related to Windows Store app development. If you instead wish to learn about the new APIs in Windows 8.1, you can refer to the MSDN documentation.

 *Tip: XAML IntelliSense improvements discussed in Chapter 4 are certainly valid for Windows 8.1 app development. Since I already talked about such improvements in detail before, I will not repeat them here.*

## New project templates

Windows 8.1 introduces a new control called **Hub**, which provides the ability to create a central hub in your Windows Store apps. Basically the concept of a hub is providing users with a landing page that gives an overview of different parts of the app in one place. Before Windows 8.1, developers had to do a bit of work to manually create a hub. To highlight the importance of this control, Visual Studio 2013 introduces the **Hub** control and a specific project template called Hub App, which is available for both XAML and HTML modes, and only if you run Visual Studio 2013 on Windows 8.1. Figure 88 shows the New Project dialog with the new template selected.

*Figure 88: The New Hub App Project Template*

Understanding how the **Hub** control works is very easy. You can just create a new project based on the Hub App template. When the project is ready, start the application before looking at the code. By either using the mouse or your finger, you can scroll the main page horizontally to see how the Hub allows creating sections of contents or shortcuts to additional pages. Figure 89 shows the sample app running.

*Figure 89: The Hub Control allows organizing content and shortcuts.*

Now look at the XAML code. The built-in project template provides a very rich and powerful example, but what you need to know at the higher-level is represented in the following code.

```
<Hub SectionHeaderClick="Hub_SectionHeaderClick">
    <Hub.Header>
        <Grid>
        <!-- Controls here... -->
        </Grid>
    </Hub.Header>
    <HubSection Width="780" Margin="0,0,80,0">
        <HubSection.Background>
        <!-- Your brush here... -->
        </HubSection.Background>
        <Grid>
        <!-- Controls here... -->
        </Grid>
    </HubSection>
    <HubSection Width="500" Header="Section 1">
        <DataTemplate>
        <!-- Your data-bound items here... -->
        </DataTemplate>
    </HubSection>
```

```
      </Hub>
```

Among the others, the **Hub** control exposes the **Header** property that shows content summarizing the topic of the section. Because of the XAML hierarchical nature, **Header** can be not only text, but also a set of nested controls. The **Hub** control contains **HubSection** controls for as many topics as you need to summarize. The **HubSection** control is very versatile, since it can store any kind of content. As you can see from the code snippets in the previous listing, you can put text or panels, set the background, and even place data-bound controls via **DataTemplate** elements. The MSDN Code Gallery contains a very good example of the **Hub** control for both XAML and HTML that you can download for additional testing. Of course, the MSDN documentation provides everything you need to know for building apps with the **Hub** control. Since explaining how to program this control in detail is beyond the scope of this book, you can check out the related page on MSDN.

# Improved Device tool window

When you work with the designer on a Windows Store app, you can take advantage of a useful tool window called Device (also known as Device panel). It allows changing some properties of your application so that you can get a preview of your edits at design time, avoiding the need to launch the application every time. The Device panel is not new in Visual Studio 2013; it was already available in Visual Studio 2012, but has now been reorganized and updated with new features. Figure 90 shows the Device panel.

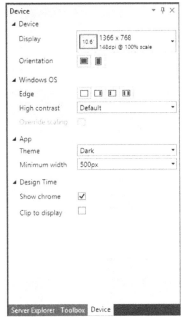

*Figure 90: The Device Tool Window*

Properties on the window are self-explanatory, and it's easy to see the result on the designer when you change them. In summary you can:

- Change the app resolution in the designer with the Display property.
- Switch between horizontal and vertical orientation with the Orientation property.
- Test how the app will appear on screen with the Edge property.
- Select the screen contrast with the High contrast property.
- Test the app on a different scaling with the Override scaling property. Scaling is increased by 40%.
- Change the theme to see how the app responds to system settings with the Theme property.
- Establish a minimum app width with the Minimum width property
- Show or remove the device chrome in the designer with the Chrome property.
- Clip the entire document or show the document display with the Clip to display property.

The Device panel is a good companion to get a preview of the behavior of the app directly in the designer, so that you can change the app layout and appearance and see if the result you get is what you (and your users) expect.

# Connect to Windows Azure mobile services

In Chapter 5, you discovered new features in the Server Explorer window to provide integration with Windows Azure services from within the IDE. You learned what a mobile service is and how to create one from Server Explorer. Continuing the integration with the cloud platform, Visual Studio 2013 allows connecting easily to a mobile service in Windows 8.1 applications.

In a Store app, first save the project—otherwise the tooling will not work without giving you any warning. Then right-click the project name in Solution Explorer, then select **Add**, **Connected Service**. At this point the Services Manager dialog appears. Select the **Windows Azure** node to see a list of available services, as shown in Figure 91.

*Figure 91: The Services Manager dialog shows available Mobile Services.*

Once you click **OK**, a service reference is added. Visual Studio 2013 will automatically add references to assemblies that are required in order to connect to the service in code and to manage data stored inside the service. You can expand the **References** node in Solution Explorer to see what libraries have been referenced; Figure 92 demonstrates this.

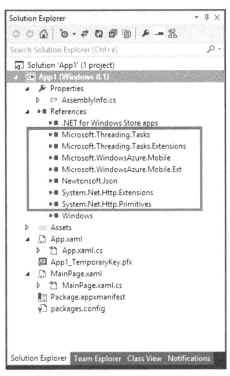

Figure 92: References Added to Support Coding against Mobile Services

The new assemblies required to interact with a Mobile Service are Microsoft.WindowsAzure.Mobile.dll and Microsoft.WindowsAzure.Mobile.Ext.dll. Other assemblies are part of the .NET runtime and are required for serializing and deserializing data through the JSON format over the network. Not limited to this, Visual Studio 2013 will also add to the **App** class code the following line (**yourmobileservice** stands for the name of your service and **YOURSECRETKEY** stands for the client secret key, both added appropriately):

*Visual C#*

```
public static Microsoft.WindowsAzure.MobileServices.MobileServiceClient
yourmobileserviceClient = new
Microsoft.WindowsAzure.MobileServices.MobileServiceClient(
        "https://yourmobileservice.azure-mobile.net/",
        "YOURSECRETKEY");
```

*Visual Basic*

```
Public Shared yourmobileserviceClient As New
Microsoft.WindowsAzure.MobileServices.MobileServiceClient(
        "https://yourmobileservice.azure-mobile.net/",
        "YOURSECRETKEY");
```

By creating an instance of the
**Microsoft.WindowsAzure.MobileServices.MobileServiceClient** class, your app will be
able to connect to the specified mobile service. For a deeper understanding of the code you
need to write to manage data and C.R.U.D. operations from your app, you can follow the
example shown in the Getting started with Mobile Services page in the Windows Azure
documentation, which also provides guidance to use these services in other platforms.

## Asynchronous debugging

Visual Studio 2013 introduces a new tool window called Tasks, which helps developers debug
asynchronous operations written according to the Async/Await pattern introduced with the
previous version. This feature was discussed in detail in the previous chapter, so you should be
able to use it successfully against Windows Store apps.

## Analyze performance with the XAML UI Responsiveness Tool

Visual Studio 2013 brings to XAML Store apps the UI Responsiveness Tool that was already
available for HTML/JavaScript Store applications. As the name implies, this tool analyzes the
user interface performance and generates a detailed report about the app behavior. In order to
use this tool, you need to open the Performance and Diagnostics Hub that you discovered in the
previous chapter. When visible, you have to select the **XAML UI Responsiveness** check box,
as shown in Figure 93.

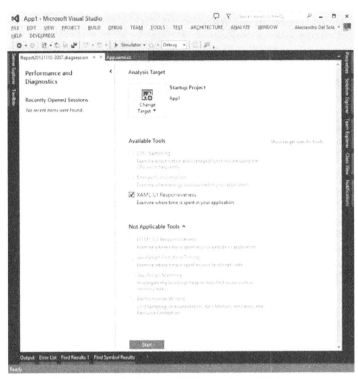

*Figure 93: Selecting the XAML UI Responsiveness Tool*

When ready, click the **Start** button. Use your app for a while, then close it or go back to Visual Studio and click the **Stop Collection** hyperlink. After a few seconds, Visual Studio shows a detailed report about the collected information about performances; Figure 94 shows an example.

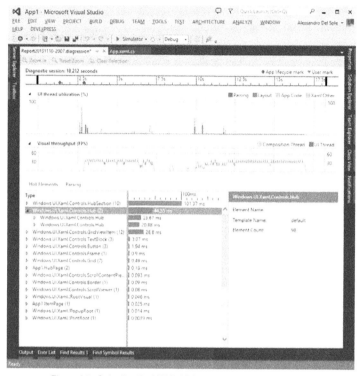

*Figure 94: Selecting the XAML UI Responsiveness Tool*

The report can be divided into four main parts. Let's discuss them in more detail.

## Diagnostic Session

The Diagnostic Session report shows information about the application lifecycle and user interaction. It displays the test duration and it shows how much time the app required for activation. This section can be useful to discover important performance problems that you must avoid for a successful app submission.

## UI Thread Utilization

The UI Thread Utilization section shows how the UI thread has been exploited in percentage by different tasks managed by the runtime. You can understand how many resources have been consumed by the XAML parser (blue), how many in rendering the user interface (dark orange), in executing the app code (light green), and in other tasks related to XAML (not parsing). This can be very useful to understand what areas of your code have the most negative impact on the overall performance.

## Visual Throughput (FPS)

This section shows how many frames per second (FPS) have been rendered during the application lifecycle; for timing, you can take the Diagnostic Session as a reference. This tool is very straightforward, and can show frames in both the UI thread and the composition thread. If you pass the mouse pointer over the graphic, you will see a tooltip showing frames per second for both threads at the given time.

 *Tip: If you are new to Windows Store application development, you might not be familiar with the concept of composition thread. The composition thread was introduced with Windows Phone and is a companion thread for the UI thread, in that it does some work that the UI thread would normally do. The composition thread is normally responsible for combining graphics texture and for sending them to the GPU for rendering. This is all managed by the runtime; by invoking the composition thread, the runtime can make an app stay much more responsive and you, as the developer, will not need to do any additional work.*

## Hot Elements and Parsing

At the bottom of the report, you will find two tabs, **Hot Elements** and **Parsing**. Hot Elements shows the list of UI elements (.NET objects with their fully qualified name) and the time in milliseconds they have been busy with the application execution. Objects in the list can be expanded to show nested controls and types. When you click an object, you will also be able to see additional information such as nested elements count, XAML code file (if not a system object), and the control template, on the right side of the window. The Parsing tab shows the list of XAML files in the application package and how much time in milliseconds has been required for parsing. This tool is not limited to XAML files you see in Solution Explorer, but also works against built-in XAML files prepackaged in the application.

## Chapter summary

Windows 8.1 is the new major upgrade for the Windows 8 operating system, which introduces tons of new APIs and features that developers can leverage to build amazing apps. Visual Studio 2013 is the environment you need to build apps for Windows 8.1. This new version introduces a new **Hub** control, which Visual Studio 2013 supports with the Hub App project template. At design time, you can get previews of your app's look and feel via the Device panel. You can now easily connect to Windows Azure Mobile Services and Visual Studio will do most of the work for you. Great apps are fluid and fast apps, so with Visual Studio 2013 you have a new analysis tool called XAML UI Responsiveness, which helps you understand how and where your app spends more time and consumes more resources.

www.ingramcontent.com/pod-product-compliance
Lightning Source LLC
Chambersburg PA
CBHW071255050326
40690CB00011B/2403